The Good
Working Mother's Guide

Mary Beard

Duckworth

First published in 1989 by
Gerald Duckworth & Co. Ltd.
The Old Piano Factory
43 Gloucester Crescent, London NW1

ISBN 0 7156 2278 1

British Library Cataloguing in Publication Data

Beard, Mary
  The good working mother's guide
  1. Great Britain. Children. Home care.
  Nannies. 2. Great Britain. Working mother.
  Children. Day care
  I. Title
  649'.1

  ISBN 0-7156-2278-1

Photoset in North Wales by
Derek Doyle & Associates, Mold, Clwyd.
Printed and bound in Great Britain by
Redwood Burn Limited, Trowbridge

Contents

Thanks

Working mothers learn the tricks of the trade from other working mothers. Many of my friends and colleagues will see their own experiences (and disasters) reflected in this book. I am grateful to them all.

Particular thanks are due to my own mother, Sarah Beard (most of all, for proving that working motherhood was possible); to Ros Egan and Clare Smith (for giving the nannies' inside story); to Claire Millett and Jan Walker (for discussing childminding and nurseries); to Shantelle Millie (for searching out some of the background information); to Raymond Thomas (for help on money); to Isabel Boucher (for the drawing); to Sophie Cormack (for reading and improving the whole text); and to Robin Cormack (for being a more helpful partner than this book anticipates!).

He or she?

Writers of books on childcare can go to extreme lengths to avoid the accusation of sexism. They resolutely refer to the baby as 'she' – or even use 'she' and 'he' alternately from one chapter to the next. I have followed no such system. I have simply written with my own experience in mind.

When I was preparing this book, I had a tiny baby son and a daughter a little bit older. So when I refer to babies I tend to say 'he' – when I mean toddlers in particular, 'she'. The same goes for the other people in the book. My GP and my nanny are both female; my accountant and obstetrician male. And that's how they normally appear in the text. But all these genders are reversible according to the reader's own experience.

The same is true for 'mother'. There is much in the book that would be useful to working, and especially single, fathers. They should read 'father' for 'mother' throughout – except in the sections on pregnancy and breastfeeding!

For Sarah, Robin, Zoe, Raphael and Ros

Introduction

This is a book about *choosing* and *using* childcare. It is not a book about 'maternal deprivation', 'bonding', or the emotional needs of mothers and young children. Most important, it is not a book about *guilt*. Many other writers have had a lot to say on all these subjects – especially guilt! You will have to decide for yourself about the psychological advantages and disadvantages of working motherhood. You will also have to decide for yourself whether you can *afford* to give up your job. This book assumes that you've come through those dilemmas – and that you are intending to go back to full-time work soon after the birth of your baby. Or perhaps you are already there. It aims to give you the basic information you will need to make a success of (and enjoy!) what is still a rare combination: having a full-time job *and* being the mother of young children.

The book is written with the needs of *full-time* working mothers most in mind. There is, of course, a lot in it that will be useful to part-timers. But it doesn't look at those options in childcare that might particularly suit someone with part-time work – but would be next to useless for those of us who have to be at our jobs for 40 hours a week most of the year. So you will find almost no information here on au pairs, morning playgroups or baby-sitting services.

You will also find that the book concentrates on the needs of children up to the age of three. This is not because things necessarily get easier then. In some respects it is more difficult to arrange childcare for kids who are at school half the year. Never underestimate the trouble you can have with a strongminded six-year-old – who has her own firm views on what she wants to do between the end of school and the time you come home! But all the same, those problems are very different from the problems you face in organising day-care for a child who is still not old enough to explain to you his likes and dislikes. This book is about the care of babies and toddlers – the ones who won't be able to tell you when something's going wrong. It's an even greater responsibility.

The cynical advice to a working woman starting a family would be – move abroad! Britain has a worse record on maternity rights and subsidised childcare than any other country in the EEC. And we have a smaller proportion of mothers of young children at work than in the rest of the Community. In fact only 6 per cent of women in Britain with kids under three years old have a full-time job (though many more have part-time work).

Imagine we were in France. There would be no fear that we would lose our jobs just because we were pregnant, and we would continue to receive full pay right through our maternity leave. And as for the children – we would find a third of all two-year-olds in state-funded day-care, and almost 90 per cent of three-year-olds.

Compare that with the UK. Around half of British women at work have no right to keep their job when they have a baby. And the top rate of Statutory Maternity Pay (for which many women don't qualify) is only 90 per cent of your normal wage for just six weeks. The picture is equally gloomy when it comes to childcare. Only 1 per cent of children under three are in day nurseries sponsored by local councils. So what happens to the children of that 6 per cent of full-time working mothers? Over half are cared for by a relative – grandmother, aunt or father. This isn't because we in Britain have particularly close, loving families who *want* to take on this responsibility. It is simply that the cost of private childcare is out of reach of many of the lowest-paid working women.

Britain also lags behind in giving women any positive encouragement to keep their jobs when they start a family. A few private firms, it is true, have devised imaginative schemes to help women stay in their jobs over those first, difficult few years with a young child. But, as a country, we take nothing like the initiative of our European neighbours. In Holland, for example, they have recently designed a special uniform for pregnant policewomen. When was the last time you saw a pregnant policewoman here? You probably never have! They normally have to leave the force when they get pregnant.

These brutal facts on maternity rights and childcare are not simply meant to enrage you – though you certainly should protest about this dreadful state of affairs whenever and wherever you can. They are meant to provide you with essential background information for embarking on working motherhood. They are meant to reassure you that you are *not* being hopelessly inefficient if you find it hard to get a nursery place for your baby. There really aren't enough places to go round. And you're *not* being paranoid if you occasionally feel that the world is organised for the convenience of everyone but you. Working mothers are in a tiny minority. Most people won't expect you to have a small baby and a full-time job – least of all the telephone engineer or the gasman, who will always assume you can wait in for them all day!

On the other hand, don't let the facts and figures make you despondent. That tiny 6 per cent amounts to almost 200,000 mothers. They all *do* manage to find some kind of satisfactory childcare. Some of it is far from ideal. Some of it seems very expensive. But some of it is first-rate. A substantial proportion of working mothers feel entirely happy with the arrangements they have made for their children – and never regret for one minute the decision to go on working. To put it bluntly – money is what is important. If you have a job with a reasonable salary, you will actually find you have quite a *choice* on the private childcare market.

NANNIES FIRST?

The biggest section of the book is about private nannies. This may seem, at first, a little odd. After all, very few women have nannies – while over half take their children to granny or another relative. Why doesn't the book reflect this situation?

The reasons are clear. First of all – no book can tell you about your own family. If you happen to have a sister or a mother who is willing to look after your child, then you may be very lucky. But only *you* can know what the advantages and disadvantages will be. Only *you* can know whether it is an offer worth accepting. It is the same with partners. There is no point in recommending to a working mother that she rely on her partner. Not everyone has a partner. And even those of us that do, don't find that they are always around at the time we need the help. Your family is your own affair. The more help you can get from it the better. But this book assumes that you are relying on outside (paid) help.

But why look at nannies first, out of all the options in outside care? For the simple reason that more and more women *are* using nannies – and that this involves by far the most complicated arrangements of all forms of childcare. It involves not only *finding* a nanny, but also becoming her *employer* – with all the legal obligations that that brings with it. And it involves *trusting* the person you find to an even greater extent than you must trust a nursery or childminder. After all the nanny is going to be *on her own* with the child for the whole working day – and no one else will be there to see what is going on. There's no 'community of parents' for you to share your worries with. You have to be able to feel confident that you have got the right person.

For these reasons nannies get the most space. But much of the advice in the 'nanny chapters' applies to other forms of childcare as well – and is not repeated in the sections on childminders and nurseries. So even if you are certain that you are looking for a nursery place for your child – you should still read through the earlier chapters. Lots of the discussion will be relevant to you.

WHY READ THIS BOOK?

Childcare is a subject for which you *must* do some reading in advance. There are lots of other areas of life where books are simply no substitute for 'having a go'. Why read a book on how to swim – when you can go to your local pool and see if you like it? Childcare is different. For the sake of the child, you can't chop and change until you finally come up with an arrangement that suits you. Even if *you* don't think your childminder is really satisfactory, your toddler will have made an emotional commitment to her. You shouldn't wrench him away just to try out a nursery that may, or may not, be better.

This book aims to give you some of the information that you *would* get from experience! It will help you decide which option in childcare is best for you. Of course you will still need a good deal of luck. No working mother has a trouble-free life – it would be quite dishonest to claim otherwise. But this book will certainly make sure that your troubles are fewer!

1

Before the birth: a working pregnancy

Very few women want to sit at home 'taking it easy' throughout their pregnancy. Even fewer can afford to! On the other hand, it can be exhausting doing a full-time job, particularly in the early months of your pregnancy. And most ante-natal care seems to assume that you have no commitments in your life other than growing a baby. How are you going to manage if you do decide to work through your pregnancy? And, more important, is it safe – for you and the baby?

SAFETY AT WORK

You will get all kinds of conflicting advice on whether it is safe to work while you are pregnant. It is sensible to consider the problem in two parts – first, whether there are any *specific hazards* in your job (such as dangerous chemicals or radiation); secondly, whether the strains and stresses of *simply having a job* (travelling to work, not always being able to rest when you want to) are dangerous to the health of you and your child.

Specific hazards

Legal rules

For some working women the hazards of employment are well-known and sometimes legally recognised. Radiographers must avoid exposure to radiation. And other women whose work may involve contact with X-rays should certainly not continue with that type of job while expecting a baby. This exposure can happen in a wide variety of occupations – the cigarette industry (where radiation may be used for thickness gauges), certain types of security operation (though not standard airport security), even commercial Christmas pudding manufacture (where X-rays have been used for testing!).

Legal restrictions are also imposed on women working in the lead industry or in processes that use large quantities of lead. In some areas (such as lead smelting and battery making) no woman at all is allowed to take a job. In others, women 'of reproductive capacity' are allowed a much lower limit of exposure to lead than male workers. And pregnant women are given a lower limit still, or banned entirely.

All these rules are designed mainly to protect the unborn child from damage. But remember that the worst damage is likely to occur in very early pregnancy, before you are likely to know (or to be sure) that you are pregnant. So it is important to think early about these major risks – if possible, before there is any chance that you are pregnant.

Other chemical hazards

Many other substances, too many to list in full, have been associated with damage to the growing foetus, with low birth weight, premature delivery and other reproductive problems – such as an increased tendency to miscarry or infertility. A large number of different types of job may be affected. Hospital workers, for example, may be at risk from exposure to a range of different chemicals. Anaesthetic gases have been linked to an increased risk of miscarriage among staff of operating theatres and some sterilising agents (notably hexachlorophene and ethylene oxide) have been associated with malformations of the baby or miscarriages. Likewise any woman handling mercury, benzene (common in dyes and solvents), toluene (used in electrical insulation), arsenic, dioxin and organochlorines (all common ingredients of pesticides) or vinyl chloride (used to make PVC) – to name just a few – may endanger the health of her baby.

If you work with any chemicals at all you should talk to your trade union health and safety officer, preferably before you become pregnant. You should be aware of the potential dangers of your workplace as soon as possible. But you should also remember that it is very difficult to assess accurately the risks of any particular substance to the pregnant woman and her child. Even in the case of some of the better known 'dangerous substances' listed above, it is by no means certain what the real dangers are. It is particularly difficult to isolate the risks of any one individual substance among all the possible hazards of a workplace and all the possible social, environmental or psychological factors. So, for example, some authorities (including the Royal College of Obstetricians and Gynaecologists) have questioned the dangers of exposure to anaesthetic gases. They have argued that any increased risk of miscarriage to women working in operating theatres is to be explained by anxiety (that is the stressful atmosphere, and even worry over the possible dangers of the gases) rather than by a direct chemical effect of the anaesthetic itself. This is a very difficult area of science. We could only reach a certain conclusion if we were to expose pregnant women selectively to suspected hazardous substances. Most people would find that an unacceptable experiment.

VDUs

Particular uncertainty still surrounds the safety of visual display units (VDUs) on word processors and computer terminals. These are used by hundreds of thousands of women in secretarial jobs, journalism, travel agency and many other occupations. Any risk to pregnancy caused by these machines could affect a substantial proportion of working mothers. The first well publicised suggestion of danger from VDUs came from Canada, where in one year four women working on VDUs at the offices of the *Toronto Star* gave birth to babies with moderate to severe handicaps.

Similar clusters were noticed in other places in North America. So, for example, between 1980 and 1981, at the Old City Hall in Toronto, over half the pregnancies of VDU operators ended in miscarriage.

There came also to be similar worries in Britain. Women operators of VDUs in the Department of Employment at Runcorn were shown to have a 36 per cent rate of miscarriage, still-birth or birth defect (compared with an average of 16 per cent amongst the other non-VDU users). And at a bank in Grimsby in the late 1970s five pregnancies out of five among VDU users ended abnormally – in either miscarriage, still-birth or handicap.

It is not yet clear how reliable these figures are or how they might be explained. Some research claims that the VDUs themselves are dangerous to pregnant women, perhaps giving off a small level of radiation sufficient to damage the foetus. Others (including a recent study by the Royal College of Obstetricians and Gynaecologists) suggest there is no serious danger at all. Still others have suggested that it is not the machines themselves that are dangerous, but the tiring and stressful conditions under which many VDU operators work. This is not just the strain of the flickering screen or normal typist's bad posture. Some companies program the machines to monitor electronically how quickly the woman works, how accurate she is and how often she leaves her work station. It is as if her boss was *constantly* at her shoulder, watching her *every* move!

If you want to be absolutely on the safe side, you should ask your employers to transfer you to a 'non-VDU environment' while you are pregnant – and, if possible, while you are trying to conceive. This option of transfer is recommended in the TUC guidelines on the use of VDUs. It has also been confirmed by an industrial tribunal, which found in favour of a woman who claimed that she had been unfairly dismissed for insisting on non-VDU work while pregnant. The tribunal upheld her claim because her fears about the dangers were, they decided, 'by no means ill-founded'.

Hazards in perspective

It is important to be aware of the many dangers to yourself and your baby that you may find in your workplace. But don't get the various 'pregnancy scares' out of perspective. Television and newspapers like nothing more than a good story about yet another unsuspected danger to the developing child. In recent years airport noise, excessive heat and ultrasound scanning in industry have all been blamed by the media for various birth defects. But scientific analysis has not confirmed the dangers. Even where some clear link has been established between a particular substance and certain types of abnormality or illness in the child, the risk may still be very small indeed. For most of us exposure to chemical or physical dangers is by no means the most important factor in our ability to bear healthy children. Our annual income and standard of living, and the unpredictable genetic make-up of the baby have a much bigger part to play in ensuring a successful pregnancy.

The general hazards of a working life

Some people (including some doctors) would claim that the strains and stresses of simply *being at work* are not good for the health of the pregnant woman and her baby – quite apart from any specific chemical or physical hazard. Research on this issue is conflicting and inconclusive. And not surprisingly it has proved difficult to isolate the effects of work itself from the complex social and financial factors that set working women apart from their non-working counterparts. All kinds of conclusions have been drawn from the various research projects in Britain and abroad. Some studies have suggested that working women have a smaller chance of giving birth prematurely than those that do not work. Others have suggested exactly the reverse. Some have shown a correlation between mothers who work late into their pregnancy and babies of low birth weight. Others have been able to demonstrate no such correlation at all. Nothing seems firmly established.

It is not, of course, surprising, if you think about it, that the research results are so conflicting. It is very hard to make any fair comparison between the very broad categories of 'working' and 'non-working' women. 'Work' for one woman is not the same as 'work' for another. And 'not having paid employment', as defined in social statistics, is by no means the same as 'not working'. It would be difficult to argue, for example, that a woman employed doing research in a library was undergoing the same physical stress as a shopworker or nurse – or, for that matter, as a mother at home officially 'not working', with two children under three!

The best advice is: if you are happy working, then continue. It is far better to stay at work than to sacrifice your pay and lose the companionship and interest of your job – just because you feel somehow that you *ought* to stop work. But if you are exhausted after a strenuous day's work and perhaps a tiring journey at either end – then *stop*.

TIMING YOUR LEAVE

It is very hard to predict when you will want to give up work. Some women feel perfectly fit and full of energy right up to the day they give birth. Others are flagging by thirty weeks. You cannot know for certain at the outset which category you will fall into. Even if it is your second pregnancy and you were still happy to be at work right up to the moment your first child was born, it will not necessarily be the same this time.

Rights to maternity leave differ. They will depend on your organisation and on how long you have been in your job. The main lines of these complicated arrangements are summarised in the next chapter. But as a guiding principle there is just one simple rule: if you have an entitlement to leave, do not go on working longer than *you* want just because you feel guilty about letting your colleagues down. Martyrs do not make good mothers. Maternity leave is given to you because you *need* it – and if you work too long, you will only end up resenting your job and your misplaced loyalty to your colleagues. From your own point of view you will need to think in advance about the financial consequences of being absent, the kind of work you do and the various factors that are likely to affect your energy and feelings towards the end of your pregnancy.

For many women the financial costs of giving up work at the earliest possible moment will weigh heavily. Your period of leave on full pay, or close to full pay, is bound to be limited (for details, see pp. 31-6). If you can go on happily working and earning, there is no point in giving up your job and claiming your paid leave – only to be forced to take unpaid leave (or leave on much reduced pay) later. Besides, many women (if they have a choice) would prefer to take the bulk of their leave after the birth of the baby. That way, they have more time to get to know the new arrival and they might get through the worst of the broken nights before they have to return to work. Your decision here is likely to depend very much on the particular rights to leave that apply in your organisation. But you must also bear in mind the kind of job you have. It is difficult (and not advisable) to keep going late into pregnancy if you have a very tiring job, particularly one that keeps you on your feet all day. Sitting at an office desk when you are thirty-eight weeks pregnant is one thing. Serving in a shop or a restaurant is quite another.

Some pregnancies are predictably going to be more tiring than others. If you are expecting twins, you should certainly not *plan* to work up to the fortieth week of your pregnancy. You are likely to be bigger, more uncomfortable, and to suffer more of the minor complications of pregnancy than someone expecting just a single baby. And you may well deliver before the end of your forty weeks – the average length of a twin pregnancy being less than thirty-eight weeks.

Having a young toddler about the house may also make a difference to whether you feel like carrying on with your job very close to your expected date of confinement. People often say that second and later pregnancies are easier than the first, and in many ways they are. But people also tend to forget the sheer exhaustion involved in looking after your other children. It is not, like the first time you were pregnant, a question of just struggling home from work and then putting your feet up. It is struggling home from work, and then mounting the energy to cook the children's supper, bath them and get them off to bed. And the weekends too are likely to mean a frantic series of games, potties, trips to the park and the zoo – not like the first time round, when you could lie in bed till late and curl up with a book for most of the afternoon. The best advice for most people in this situation is to give up work before you reach the absolute end of your tether. Keep on your childcare arrangements if at all possible, and give yourself some time *to yourself* before the next onslaught!

Whenever you decide to give up work, you may have to change your plans at the last minute. Various complications towards the end of your pregnancy may mean that it would be impossible (or at least very foolish) to continue at your job. If you develop high blood pressure, for example, you will almost certainly be advised to take things easy. If you turn up at the ante-natal clinic one morning with rocketing blood pressure and traces of protein in your urine, you will be told to rest (whether at home or in hospital) *straight away*. In these circumstances you will almost certainly have to give up work. There is no need to worry about not being able to give your employers the three weeks' notice normally required (see pp. 28, 34). If it is early in your pregnancy, take sick leave. If it is towards the end, simply inform your employers that you will be taking maternity leave straight away. The law exempts you from the three-week requirement if it is not 'reasonably practicable' to give it.

TELLING YOUR EMPLOYERS

Almost as difficult as deciding when to stop work is deciding when to tell your employers that you are expecting a baby. If you are certain of your maternity rights, you should tell them almost as soon as your pregnancy is confirmed. You will need their cooperation in arranging your paid absences for ante-natal care. And besides, if they are to support *you* in getting your proper maternity rights, it is only reasonable that you should help *them* by giving them good advance warning that you will be absent. You should ask them to treat your news in confidence, if you do not want your pregnancy to become common knowledge immediately.

The decision on when to inform your employers will not of course be so easy, if you do not fulfil the qualifying period for job security and other maternity rights (see pp. 26-7, 31-5). It might be best to tell your employers early and give yourself plenty of time to negotiate with them for the option to return to work later. But that course of action does carry risks. Your employers might decide to dismiss you immediately!

TELLING YOUR COLLEAGUES

There is also no perfect time to tell your colleagues, but advantages and disadvantages whenever you choose. If you are in a job where plans (for work allocation and responsibilities) are made a long way in advance, you may well decide to tell them from the very beginning. This is probably better than solemnly pretending that you will be happy to teach French to the Upper Fourth next year, when you know all the time that you will be at home with the nappies for most of the first term! It also has the added advantage that you may gain some sympathy and real help from your colleagues in those early months, when you may feel absolutely ghastly but show no visible signs of your condition. On the other hand, if you have an early miscarriage (and miscarriages are common up to the twelfth week of pregnancy), you will be faced with the added emotional burden of telling everyone that you are *no longer* pregnant. If you delay your announcement, you will have to struggle through the difficult early months with a variety of barely convincing excuses for being 'off colour'. But at least by the time you finally do tell, you will be fairly confident that your pregnancy really will result in a baby.

If you are going to have an amniocentesis, there may be an additional reason for delaying the announcement of your news. This test (which can detect abnormalities such as Down's syndrome and spina bifida) is commonly carried out for women over the age of thirty-five, when the risk of particularly a Down's baby rises sharply (see p. 21). It is performed around the sixteenth week of pregnancy and the full results are not known for about four weeks after that. If a major abnormality is discovered, a termination of the pregnancy is then usually offered. With this test in prospect, you will obviously feel reluctant to tell your colleagues that you are expecting a baby. You will not want to face sharing with everyone at work the difficult decision of whether or not to accept a termination. And you will not want to risk the possibility that some people will actively disapprove of your decision, if you do feel you must have a termination. No one, after all, will find you morally reprehensible if you suffer a miscarriage. Some, unhappily, will judge you guilty, if (however reluctantly) you choose to abort a foetus you know to be seriously handicapped. Faced with these uncertainties, concealing your pregnancy will probably seem the obvious option. But you must remember that by twenty weeks (the time you will probably receive the results of the test) almost all women are quite noticeably pregnant. Even if you have said nothing, people will have begun to suspect. There is almost nothing worse, when waiting for the results of your amnio, than having your colleagues furtively scrutinising your stomach when they think you're not looking.

COPING AT WORK

There are some irritating problems in being pregnant at work. Most irritating of all perhaps is the way some of your colleagues start to treat you as a 'pregnant body' not as 'you'. They will not *all* be like this, but you can almost guarantee that *some* will. Where they used chat with you about politics, football, your latest client, the weather, anything... now they will only ask you how you are 'feeling' or when the baby is due (a date, be warned, that no one will ever remember, no matter how often they have been told!).

This kind of 'pregnancy talk' is always difficult to deal with. And it is particularly hard to handle in your working environment – where (as far as you are concerned) the simple fact that you are expecting a baby should not make much difference to your job or your relations with your colleagues. I certainly found no good way to cope. When it all got too much, I found that I would lash out at whatever unfortunate individual happened to ask (yet again – and no doubt well-meaningly) 'how I was'. 'About the same as yesterday, and the day before and the day before that,' I would reply! This sarcasm made *me* feel better, but I am not sure that it had much effect on the outside world. It probably only confirmed their view that pregnant women are a little unhinged.

The best response to all this tedious interest is to try to turn it to your own advantage. You are almost bound to feel sick or tired or cumbersome (or all three) for part of your pregnancy, and you will need to adapt your conditions at work to make it manageable. If your immediate superior is so concerned about your health, then ask if you can borrow his or her office (with the big sofa!) at lunchtime, so you can snatch half an hour's sleep. Or get your friends to pick up your lunch from the snack bar and bring it back to you – rather than walk all the way over there yourself. At least that way you can convert some of the cloying interest into real help.

It will still be difficult to get the balance right. You will probably need to alter your work patterns a bit during your pregnancy, but don't overplay the 'frail woman' hand. After all you are still *working* – and if you really need to spend two hours each morning in the loo and three hours of the afternoon asleep, then honestly you should be at home. My own rule was to let my standards slip *a bit* and to do anything which, however unconventional, made it easier to go on doing the job properly. So, for example, if you feel better with your feet up at your desk, put them up – even if there are some frowns. If you feel most comfortable squatting, then squat while you are on the phone. It might raise some eyebrows, but it is not going to ruin your efficiency. If you can do your job equally well sitting on a stool as standing, put in a request for a stool. If getting in to work ten minutes late means that you miss the rush hour and can start the day with some energy left, then ask permission to start late. If a ten-minute break mid-afternoon means that you can go on at full strength till the end of the day, then ask for it. The crucial thing is to work out as far as possible in advance what is going to help you and to take positive steps to get it. And remember, most women are more conscientious than most men, so taking things a bit easy will only bring you down to the normal male level!

ANTE-NATAL CARE

Midwives, doctors and clinics

The organisation of ante-natal care in this country seems to assume that from the moment you get pregnant you will have a full-time commitment to motherhood. Ante-natal clinics typically run block appointments (so that you and five other women are all booked in for 10.30!) and have legendary long waiting times that make normal out-patients departments look speedy. Then midwives will expect to be able to visit you at home during the day – and may be as reluctant as the telephone engineer or gasman to specify an exact time for their visit. In some ways your legal right to paid time off work for ante-natal care works against you. From 'their' point of view, your work will allow you to spend all afternoon at the clinic. That is fine if your job is a sheer grind, less fun than sitting in the clinic with a book all afternoon. But it may be difficult to speed things up, if you have complicated commitments that will be hopelessly (and needlessly) upset if you are still waiting to see a doctor two hours after you arrive.

So what can you do? The best advice is to *plan ahead* with the help of your GP. As soon as you are fairly sure that you are pregnant, go and discuss with her (or him) the whole arrangement of your ante-natal care. She will be a crucial figure not only in your pregnancy, but also when you have a young baby. So if she is not sympathetic, find a new doctor straight away. If she is helpful, you will be able to get some of the following points sorted out.

• Whether or not you decide to have your baby in hospital (and almost all women do), make sure that your ante-natal care will be *shared* between the hospital clinic and your GP and/or a community midwife. This should mean fewer visits to the clinic, which is by far the most aggravating part of the whole ante-natal process.

- Choose your consultant carefully. Most women will be assigned to the care of one of the obstetric consultants at their local hospital. You may not see him (or her) very often, but his attitudes will make a difference to the attitudes of his subordinates. Don't get assigned at random. You may find yourself under the man who strongly disapproves of women working in pregnancy – and will order immediate bed rest if your blood pressure so much as touches 130/85. (If you don't understand the significance of this figure now, you soon will after a few visits to the hospital!) Or he might have the biggest and least punctual clinic in the whole hospital. So talk to your GP, and to your friends, about the different obstetricians available, and ask her to refer you specially to the man or woman of your choice – even, if necessary, if it involves going to a different hospital, slightly further away. I became wise to this notion of *choice* in my second pregnancy. With the help of my GP, I got referred to someone who was, from my point of view, the *perfect* consultant. I saw him himself on each of my visits to the hospital; he always asked for my views and preferences where any decision had to be made; and I never had to wait more than ten minutes!

- Your GP will probably tell your local community midwife that you are pregnant. This midwife is likely to do some of your ante-natal checks, as well as visit you during the first days the baby is at home. Ask your GP to tell her that you work, and that she should ring you *before* she makes her first visit, to arrange a time convenient to you both. The community midwife is going to be an important person in your pregnancy, who will often have much more time to discuss any problems than the midwives in a busy clinic. Make sure that you have good relations with her. But make sure that she realises right from the start that you have full-time commitments outside the home.

- Particularly if it is your second (or later) pregnancy, you may want to discuss different ways of organising your care

– with even less involvement with the hospital clinic. This need not necessarily be a complete home birth, but could be a so-called Domino scheme or birth in a GP unit at the local hospital. In the first case your care will be divided between your GP and your community midwife, who will take you to hospital when your labour starts, deliver the baby and (if all is well) take you back home six hours after the delivery. In the second, the care is divided in much the same way, and your baby will be delivered by your GP (or a midwife) in either a small local hospital or a special unit in a larger one. Both these arrangements give you the advantages of a hospital delivery (expert back-up on hand for you or the baby; someone else to clear up the mess; freedom to yell without disturbing the neighbours) – but at the same time offer a less bureaucratic approach to ante-natal care and continuity through to the delivery.

However much you have planned in advance, attending the ante-natal clinic at your hospital will still probably have its irritating sides. Long delays remain only too likely – as well as aggravating conventions such as calling everyone 'Mrs' (whether they are or not), and the patronising 'Dear'. You may feel that it is easiest just to give in to this. But it is probably better (for you and everyone who comes after you) to put up some sort of fight. Be polite, but firm. If you have waited so long that you are going to miss an important appointment at the office, tell the sister in charge of the clinic. She may be able to slip you in quickly (not necessarily queue-jumping – they might simply have been forgotten about you, or called for you when you were in the loo!). Explain to them, if necessary, that you are not *Mrs* Smith, but Miss, Ms, Dr or whatever. Correct them, each time they get in wrong. Eventually someone will write it clearly in your notes! Also, be street-wise and adopt sensible precautionary tactics. It is asking for trouble to make your appointment for 11.45. They will have had plenty of time to get behind by then. Book in at 9.00 – and get there ten minutes early, so that you are at least *morally* ahead of the four other people booked in for the same time!

Special needs

If you are very busy you may want to consider some form of private ante-natal care. This will be a particularly attractive option if you are self-employed – for, without the right to paid time off for ante-natal care, you may be losing money each hour you sit waiting in the clinic. Private appointments with a consultant obstetrician will probably involve much less waiting and can often be made outside your normal working hours. This will of course be an expensive option. Even if you have private medical insurance anyway, it will not cover private care in normal pregnancy (although the most generous schemes may cover you for medical *complications* of pregnancy – when you become in their terms 'ill'). But remember that you can opt just for private ante-natal appointments with a consultant, without going for the huge expense of a private *delivery* in a private hospital (or private wing of an NHS hospital).

For some working women ante-natal tests (checking for foetal handicap) may seem particularly important. Of course, every woman dreads bearing a handicapped child. But suppose you know that it will not be feasible (for financial reasons or whatever) for you to give up your job and that you will always be dependent on some form of childcare. Suppose also that (like many 'career women') you are having a baby in your mid-thirties, when the risk of Down's syndrome, in particular, rises sharply (to one in just over a hundred babies by the age of forty). You may then feel specially concerned to take all reasonable steps to check that the baby you are carrying does not suffer from a major handicap.

Many tests are available, and the policy on routine screening for different handicaps varies from hospital to hospital. These variations are particularly striking in the case of amniocentesis, which (by analysing a sample of the amniotic fluid surrounding the baby) can detect both spina bifida and Down's syndrome and other chromosomal abnormalities. In some hospitals this test is routinely offered to all women over thirty-five (in addition to those with a family history of the handicaps concerned). In others you will not be offered it as a matter of course unless you are thirty-seven or over.

If you specially want to have an amniocentesis you should make this clear to your GP *and* on your first visit to the hospital clinic. Don't delay. The test must be performed around the sixteenth week of your pregnancy – late enough for a clear result to be obtained, but early enough for you to be offered a termination if the test unhappily shows that a major abnormality is present. The decision to have an amniocentesis is not to be taken lightly. The test itself carries with it a small risk of miscarriage. This is only about 1 per cent overall (varying slightly from hospital to hospital) – but that is still for most younger women greater than the risk of any abnormality that the test may discover. Moreover, as most doctors will stress, it does not *guarantee* you a healthy baby. It can only reassure you that a limited range of abnormalities are not present. But if you decide that *for you* the reassurance that it offers is worth the risk, then you should certainly request the test.

You may well encounter difficulties, if you are under the age at which amniocentesis is routinely performed in your hospital. But do persevere. Point out, if you can, that at your age you would be offered the test as a matter of course at other hospitals. And remember that whatever *medical* arguments are advanced against you, the *real reasons* for fixing this or that age limit are largely financial. You may still, of course, fail to get the test – particularly if you are under thirty-five. If you are still determined to have it and can afford the high fee, you should have no difficulty in obtaining it privately. Ironically it will probably be performed by the very same man who refused you point blank on the NHS!

Preparation classes

You will find a large number of birth preparation classes on offer. Some are arranged by the hospital or by the local midwife. These are usually free. Others are run by private organisations such as women's groups or the National

Childbirth Trust (NCT). For these you will probably have to pay a small fee. It is very important to attend one course or another. You may never get the hang of the breathing exercises. You may already have decided to demand an epidural as soon as you feel the first twinge. You may be able to learn about the physiology of labour just as easily from a text-book. All the same, the classes will give you a lot of vital 'inside information' on the local hospital that you cannot so conveniently get elsewhere – from the procedures at delivery to the quality of the food and the interpretation of the visiting hours.

If your employers give you paid time off to attend classes (see p. 36), you may be tempted to go to those held in the afternoon – some private classes and most of those organised by the hospital or midwife. These may be very good. But remember that it will be difficult to take your partner at this time of day, even if, in theory, men are welcome. This means, of course, that you will miss out on his 'companionship'. But there is a more practical problem too. If you want your partner to offer you real help at the delivery, it is important that he knows what is likely to happen, what you have been taught and what kind of breathing you are *supposed* to be doing – even if you cannot remember yourself when it comes to the crunch! This is a good reason for opting for evening sessions, such as many of the NCT classes.

Bear in mind also that you are much more likely to be in a class with other working women if you choose an evening programme. That may sound a trivial reason from the outside. Childbirth is, after all, childbirth, whether you are working or not. True, of course, if you are thinking just in terms of the pains of labour. But in other respects priorities and interests do differ. It is, to say the least, alienating to find yourself in a class full of women concerned with coping at home, with escaping from the nappies, with baby-sitting circles and coffee mornings – when your main worry is how you are going to find a good child-minder in time! Full-time mothers-to-be necessarily have a different kind of commitment to pregnancy, birth and child-rearing from those who (whether they want to or not) are still at work and intend to go back to it. You will almost certainly feel more at ease if you avoid getting swamped by the 'full-timers'.

*

Most of the practical problems of a working pregnancy can be solved with a bit of common sense, forward planning and a certain amount of determination. By the end of nine months you will even have even have got on top of the ante-natal clinic! Too late for this pregnancy perhaps – but at least you will be prepared for next time round. Unfortunately common sense is not much help with the complex, and often illogical, details of your legal rights to maternity benefits and leave. The next chapter lays out the basic rules. But don't expect to get the hang of it all at first read.

2

Before the birth: your rights at work

For many women, working-motherhood is just a dream. They lose their jobs when they become pregnant and have no legal right to return to their work after having a baby. Some women are lucky enough to benefit from individual work-place agreements (see pp. 37-40), which provide more flexible arrangements for job security. But for the many who rely solely on the protection of the law (the various Employment and Employment Protection Acts) the rules are rigid and complicated. Strange as it may seem, your right not to be dismissed from your job is quite different from your right to receive maternity pay and other benefits.

This chapter looks first at the rules for keeping your job, then at your rights to maternity pay. It is not 'easy reading'! The legislation is littered with intricate conditions, qualifications and exceptions. Skip over any part that is obviously not relevant to you. And use the table on pp. 32-3. This gives a basic summary of the main conditions – and tells you when you should apply for what state benefit, to make sure you don't lose out.

What follows is, of course, only a general guide to this complicated legislation. It should give you a basic idea of rights during pregnancy and after. But for advice in relation to your own particular case, you *must* consult an expert. Try your union, your local Citizens Advice Bureau, an office of ACAS (Advisory, Conciliation and Arbitration Service) or (on benefits and payments) a local Social Security Office (see p. 41).

KEEPING YOUR JOB

Non-dismissal

You have a right in law not to be dismissed because of pregnancy, only

- if you have worked for the same employers for at least 16 hours a week for two years or more
  or
- if you have worked part-time (between 8 and 16 hours a week) for the same employers for five years or more.

This two- or five-year period is calculated by counting back from the eleventh week before your expected week of confinement (around the twenty-ninth week of your pregnancy).

In addition, your employers may dismiss you if you cannot do your job adequately while pregnant, or if it would be against the law for you to continue with your particular work while expecting a baby. But in both these cases your employers must offer you a suitable alternative job, if one is available in your organisation. Even if you are dismissed from your job at this stage, you may still have rights to return to your work after the birth of your child (see p. 29).

The main problem here is obvious – will you have worked long enough with your employers to qualify for the right? It is estimated that at least 50 per cent of pregnant women will fail to meet the conditions. Anyone can miss out. Imagine that a year ago you moved to a new, more responsible and better paid job with a different firm. Now you discover that you are pregnant. Unless your new firm has its own scheme of maternity benefits and job protection, you will have no legal right to remain at your work.

The only *regular* exception to this rule is the case of teachers and some other local government officials: if a teacher in a state school moves to another school controlled by the same Local Education Authority she is treated as if she has been in continuous employment with the same employers – and so qualifies for rights of non-dismissal despite her move. This and other technicalities (such as what happens if you have been on strike!) are discussed in a useful booklet produced by the Department of Employment: *Rules governing continuous employment and a week's pay.*

In some cases it is absolutely clear that it would be impossible (or, at least, very foolish) to continue your work while pregnant. Because of dangers to the developing foetus, an industrial code of practice prevents most women from working with lead during their pregnancy. And it is contrary to certain legal provisions (the Ionizing Radiation Regulations) for you to be exposed to more than a certain level (1 rem) of radiation between the time you declare your pregnancy and the time you give birth. This means that pregnant radiographers, for example, may be moved to administrative work, if they cannot be *guaranteed* proper protection from exposure. And, in other areas such as horseriding or work with dangerous chemicals (see pp. 7-9), few women would want to continue work, even if they were allowed to.

Other cases are, of course, rather more tricky. *You* might feel that you could continue to do your work adequately, but your boss might disagree. How do you decide? The Equal Opportunities Commission has recently taken up cases of various women dismissed solely because of their pregnancy. These have included a computer clerk, a teacher in a school for the handicapped, a baker and a care assistant at an old people's home. The principle that has emerged is this. If a *man* who takes time off work (because of *sickness*, for example) would not be dismissed from the job, then it is against the Sex Discrimination Act to dismiss a *woman* because she is *pregnant*. (See p. 42.)

Returning to work

Your right to return to your work after your baby is born depends on the same qualifying periods (two years and five years) as your right to non-dismissal; again the period is calculated back from the start of the eleventh week before the expected week of your confinement (the twenty-ninth week of pregnancy). You must still be employed by your employers at that date. It does not matter if you happen to be taking holiday or sick leave then; but if you have actually resigned your job before the twenty-ninth week, you lose all your rights to reinstatement.

In order to ensure your right to resume your job, you must provide your employers with full information in writing of your intention to take up your job again after the birth:

- You must write to them at least twenty-one days before you intend to stop work for the birth saying: that you will be absent from work to have a baby and that you intend to return to work after your absence. You must also tell your employers the expected week of your confinement, and you may be required to provide a 'certificate of expected confinement' (normally form Mat B1 which your doctor or midwife can give you fourteen weeks before the baby is due, but other written evidence may be acceptable).
- Your employers may write to you forty-nine days (or later) from the beginning of your expected week of confinement asking if you still intend to return to work. You must reply to this letter within fourteen days. You do not need to specify your date of return at this point; but you must confirm in writing that you intend to resume your job or you will lose your right to return.
- You must notify your employers in writing of the date you intend to return to work at least twenty-one days before that date.

You can return to work at any time you decide up to twenty-nine weeks after the week in which the baby was born (though remember that the law forbids you to work in a factory up to a month after the birth). There are three circumstances in which your return can be later than twenty-nine weeks after your confinement (or later than the date on which you had told your employers that you would return, if that is earlier):

- If you are ill at that date, you can postpone your return for up to four weeks. You can only do this once and you will need to produce a medical certificate.
- If you are prevented from returning by a strike or some other interruption of work, you will not lose your right to return – but will resume work as soon as is practicable after the end of the strike (in any case, not later than four weeks after it ends).
- Your employers can ask you to delay your return for up to four weeks. They must provide reasons for the delay and give you an exact new date for your return. You may not always be offered your old job back. If your employers find that it is 'not reasonably practicable' to reinstate you in exactly the same position, they are allowed to (and must) offer you a suitable alternative job 'in which the terms, conditions and location are not substantially less favourable' than those you had before the birth of your child.

There are only two circumstances in which your employers are not obliged to find you an alternative job, if you cannot be reinstated in your old job:

- If your employers had only five or fewer employees immediately before you were absent on maternity leave, they need not offer you either your old job back or a suitable alternative if it is not 'reasonably practicable'.

- Your old job may be removed by redundancy while you are absent on maternity leave. In this case your employers must offer you a suitable alternative if there is one available; but if there is not, you can legally be made redundant and may qualify for redundancy pay.

If you are dismissed during pregnancy because it would be impossible or illegal for you to continue in your job while expecting a child, you may still return to your job after the birth. You have a legal right to resume your post if (but for your dismissal) you *would have been* working two years for your employers (or five years part-time) at the beginning of the eleventh week before the expected week of confinement. In this case you should tell your employers in writing before, or as soon as possible after, your dismissal that you intend to return to work, and then follow the normal procedure for confirming your intentions and notifying them of your exact date of return.

The notion of 'suitable alternative work' is the most difficult point in all this legislation. Many employers stick to the spirit of the law – and are happy to give you your old job or a job that really is equal. But some are reluctant and may offer you an 'alternative' that *you* don't think is 'suitable'. It can be difficult to foresee this, since your employers are not obliged to tell you in advance that they will be offering a job that is different from that which you left. There is probably only one practical thing you can do to make things easier, if it turns out that you do need to complain about the job you have been offered (see pp. 40-2). Check over your job description or contract of employment before you go on leave. It may have been written years ago – make sure it describes as accurately as possible your current position and responsibilities.

There are also problems if you contemplate changing from *full-time* to *part-time work* with your employers. Many women feel that this is the most satisfactory way of returning to their jobs, at least to start with. But do you have a legal *right* to a part-time position after working full-time? And what kind of part-time job may you be offered? The answers to these questions are still unclear. Some recent decisions of industrial tribunals suggest that you *do* have a right to return to part-time work after the birth of your baby. But, in this case, you may have to accept that that job is at a lower level than the full-time one you left.

Your right to return to your job is most seriously threatened by the rule which allows small employers to dismiss a woman if it is not 'reasonably practicable' to reinstate her or to offer her a suitable alternative job. The definition of 'reasonably practicable' is about as difficult as that of 'suitable alternative'. There is little chance of much improvement here. In fact there are government plans to extend this small firms exemption to businesses with ten or fewer employees – which may affect as many as one in five working women.

MATERNITY LEAVE

Strictly speaking the Employment Acts do not give women the right to 'maternity leave'. They give instead the right to return to your job after a period of absence to have a baby, and the right to claim some maternity pay. In practice this means that those women who qualify may take up to forty weeks' leave around the time of their confinement and may claim up to eighteen weeks' maternity pay. This money is payable whether or not you intend to return to work after the birth, but it is *never* payable for more than eighteen weeks. So don't celebrate too soon when you read of your right to forty weeks' leave. Twenty-two of those weeks will be unpaid.

Maternity leave

If you qualify for the right to return to work (on the conditions listed on pp. 27-9), you may stop work eleven weeks before the expected date of the birth. You can return to your job up to twenty-nine weeks after the birth.

You don't have to take leave for this whole period. Some employers may tell you that you *must* give up work eleven weeks before your baby is expected. This is not the case. You may continue to work any time up to the birth – though you may find that, if you work very late into your pregnancy, your right to some maternity pay is threatened (see pp. 34-5). You may also return to your job any time before twenty-nine weeks, provided that you follow the procedures for notifying your employers set out above (see pp. 27-9).

A period of maternity leave may affect your other rights in your job. In principle your absence to have a baby does not count as a break in your employment. So, for example, if you become pregnant again within two years (or five for a part-time worker), you will be eligible for maternity benefits, just as if you had been working without a break; you won't need to put in *another* period of two years after the end of your leave to qualify for protection against dismissal and so forth. And your period of maternity leave can be counted as a period of service at work for certain employment rights. If, for example, you are entitled to so much pay for so many years' service, your maternity leave will be included in those years.

But for other rights and benefits your period of maternity leave may simply not count. Your employment before and after that leave is notionally 'joined together', missing out the period you spent on leave. The law here is itself unclear. But industrial tribunals have established, for example, that you cannot insist that your maternity leave is included as a period of service when you are reckoning how much holiday you are due after your return to work. And you cannot necessarily take it into account when claiming a right to sabbaticals or bonus payments. But your individual workplace agreement may give you different rights.

Maternity pay

You may be eligible for one of two types of maternity pay: Statutory Maternity Pay and Maternity Allowance.

Statutory Maternity Pay (SMP)

SMP is paid to you by your employer over eighteen weeks. There are two rates of pay:

- six weeks at 90 per cent of your average weekly earnings followed by twelve weeks at a lower rate – roughly the same as what you get on 'Income Support' or the old 'Supplementary Benefit'.
- eighteen weeks of payment all at the lower rate.

To qualify for the higher rate of SMP you must have been employed by the same employers for two years (working more than sixteen

A simplified timetable of maternity rights and benefits

1st week of pregnancy Date of your last period	2nd week	3rd week	4th week
5th week	6th week	7th week By now you may know or suspect that you are pregnant.	8th week
9th week	10th week	11th week	12th week
13th week	14th week	15th week	16th week
17th week	18th week	19th week	20th week
21st week	22nd week	23rd week	24th week
25th week (15th week before expected week of confinement). Count back from here to work out your entitlement to SMP. To claim SMP you should normally still be working to this week.	26th week (14th week before expected week of confinement). You can now get Form MatB1 from your midwife or doctor. Apply now if you are claiming Maternity Allowance.	27th week	28th week
29th week (11th week before expected week of confinement). Count back from here to work out your rights to non-dismissal and return to work. You should still be employed at the beginning of this week to ensure your right to return to work – but your period of SMP may start from this point on.	30th week (10th week before expected date of confinement). Last week for telling your employer of your absence on maternity leave (if you wish to claim your full period of SMP).	31st week	32nd week
33rd week	34th week (6th week before expected week of confinement). You must have stopped work by this point if you want to claim your full period of SMP or Maternity Allowance.	35th week	36th week

37th week	38th week	39th week	40th week (expected week of confinement). Baby born – on time!
41st week	42nd week	43rd week	44th week
45th week	46th week	47th week	48th week (8th week after birth). From this date your employer may ask you to confirm in writing that you intend to return to work. You must reply within 14 days.
49th week	50th week	51st week (11th week after birth). SMP and Maternity Allowance not paid after this week.	52nd week
53rd week	54th week	55th week	56th week
57th week	58th week	59th week	60th week
61st week	62nd week	63rd week	64th week
65th week	66th week (26th week after birth). You must normally have notified your employer by this week of the date you intend to return to work.	67th week	68th week
69th week (29th week after birth). You must normally have returned to work by this week.			

Note: you may find that you have to make adjustments to this calendar if your baby is born premature or late.

hours per week) or five years (working between eight and sixteen hours per week). This period is calculated by counting *back from the fifteenth week before the week in which the baby is due (the twenty-fifth week of your pregnancy)*. You must also earn enough to pay Class 1 National Insurance contributions.

To qualify for the lower rate of SMP you need only have been employed by the same employers for six months, counting back from the fifteenth week before the week in which the baby is due. You must also meet the same National Insurance qualifications as for the higher rate.

In both cases you must still normally be at work into the fifteenth week before the expected week of confinement. Being on holiday or on sick leave counts as work. And if you were actually dismissed from your job earlier in your pregnancy because it was illegal or impossible to do your job while expecting a child (see pp. 26-7), you may also qualify *as if* you were still at work.

To receive SMP you must inform your employers (normally in writing) of the date you want to start your leave. You should do this at least twenty-one days before you intend to be absent. You will also have to provide them with medical evidence of the date your baby is due (normally form Mat B1 – see p. 28). This evidence does not have to be submitted immediately, but may be given to your employers up to three weeks after your SMP was due to start. If your baby is born premature so that you do not have time to give your employers the full three weeks' notice, you can still claim SMP. Within three weeks of the birth, you must tell your employers that the baby has been born; and the full eighteen weeks' pay will be calculated from the week following the birth. If you stop work at the eleventh week before your expected week of confinement, then SMP will be paid from the week after you give up work for eighteen weeks – provided that you do not return to your job during that time. You can remain at work up to the seventh week before your baby is expected and still qualify for the full period of SMP, paid for eighteen weeks after you stop working. But if you work into the sixth week or later you will lose a week of SMP for each week you work. In this case, if you are entitled to the higher rate of SMP, the first six weeks will still be paid at 90 per cent of your average weekly wage. You will simply be paid the lower rate for fewer weeks.

SMP is treated as regular pay, and (if it reaches the level at which they are due) income tax and National Insurance contributions will be deducted. If you receive more generous maternity pay on a private scheme with your employers, you will not receive SMP *in addition*, above your normal salary level; your statutory pay will be incorporated into the amount you receive on your private scheme.

Maternity Allowance

Maternity Allowance may be paid to some women who are not eligible for SMP – including the self-employed, members of the armed forces and those who have resigned their jobs or changed their employers early in their pregnancy. It is paid to you by a book of orders (cashable at a post office) over a period of eighteen weeks. It is slightly less than the lower rate of SMP, but no deductions are made for tax and National Insurance.

> To qualify for Maternity Allowance you must have paid standard rate National Insurance contributions (as employed or self-employed) for twenty-six out of the last fifty-two weeks ending with the fifteenth week before the expected week of confinement.
>
> To claim Maternity Allowance if you are self-employed or no longer working during the fifteenth week before the baby is due, you should obtain form MA1 from your Social Security Office (or maternity clinic). Return this to the Social Security Office as soon as possible after the beginning of the fourteenth week before the expected week of confinement. Send with it form Mat B1 (see p. 28) and, if you are self-employed and pay your National Insurance contributions by stamping a card, also send the card. If you do not yet have form Mat B1 or cannot for any reason send your National Insurance card, do not delay sending your application. Send the documents separately later. If you put off claiming Maternity Allowance (particularly if you delay until after your baby is born), you may lose some benefit.
>
> To claim Maternity Allowance if you are still employed during the fifteenth week before the expected week of confinement, you should follow the same procedure. But, in addition, you must send form SMP 1 – which your employers will give to you if you are not eligible for SMP.
>
> Maternity Allowance is paid for the same period as SMP. If you decide to work later than the eleventh week before your baby is due, you will be sent form BM25A – which you must send back to your Social Security Office when you have stopped work so that they know when to start your payments. As with SMP, if you work into the sixth week or later before your expected week of confinement, you will lose a week's benefit for each week (or part week) that you work. If your baby is born prematurely, before your Maternity Allowance was due to start, payments will begin in the week following the week of the birth.

For most women, these regulations for maternity pay mean that it is impossible to take the full forty weeks of maternity leave. Unless your employers have a more generous scheme, you will only be able to take advantage of the full period of leave if you can afford to go without pay for twenty-two of the forty weeks. And of the eighteen paid weeks, only six will qualify for payment that is close to (but even then not equal to) a normal full-time salary. What looks like a fairly lavish entitlement of almost a year's leave around the time of your baby's birth will amount to only a few short months – if, like most working women, you *need* your pay.

TIME OFF FOR ANTE-NATAL CARE

You have the legal right to take reasonable time off work for ante-natal care without loss of pay. There is no qualifying period or other restrictions on this right. Your employers can ask to see proof of your ante-natal appointments (a hospital appointment card, for example). But you can attend your *first* appointment without providing such proof.

This ruling leaves it unclear whether or not you can take time off to attend relaxation or or birth preparation classes. Some employers are very happy for you to do this. Others are less so. An industrial tribunal has established that if you *are* given time off for this purpose, then it should be *paid* time off. But it still remains uncertain whether you are actually *entitled* to be absent for preparation classes. If you want to attend classes during working hours and you suspect your employers may not be sympathetic, you could try getting a letter from your doctor or midwife explaining that the classes are a necessary part of your ante-natal care. But remember that some classes (like those organised by the National Childbirth Trust) happen outside normal working hours. You may prefer to go to these in any case, if you want to take your partner with you (see pp. 22-3).

OUTSIDE THE LAW

Some working women are specifically excluded from most of the legislation protecting the rights of pregnant women at work. Members of the police and the armed services are not covered by the normal provisions (though they may qualify for Maternity Allowance). Also excluded from most protection are those women who normally work outside the United Kingdom according to their contract of employment, those employed in the fishing industry who are paid solely by a share of the catch (well under 20 in the whole country!) and those who work fewer than eight hours a week. You will also largely fall outside the law if you are self-employed or work freelance – whether as a dress-maker, musician, partner in a firm of solicitors or group of family doctors. You will qualify for Maternity Allowance if you have enough recent National Insurance contributions. But you will have to organise your absence from work as best you can.

Adoptive parents

Often forgotten are the needs of adoptive mothers. If you adopt a baby, you will have no statutory rights to any maternity leave or maternity pay around the time when you take the child into your home – even though, as a working mother of an adopted child, you will suffer many of the same disruptions as a 'natural' mother and will also need time to get to know your new family. But don't forget that you will be eligible for the weekly Child Benefit in just the same way as a natural parent, and some employers will have private agreements that allow you to take some (normally short) period of leave (see p. 40).

BEYOND THE LEGAL MINIMUM

There is happily another side to the gloomy picture of rigid and restricted maternity rights, as they are laid down in law. Many companies and organisations now go beyond the legal minimum and offer to their female employees more generous arrangements for job protection, maternity pay and maternity leave. These range from innovative 'career break' schemes (which enable women to return to work part-time for two or three years before resuming their full-time job) to contractual agreements which improve just slightly (whether in pay or length of leave) on what is defined by law. The varieties of these arrangements are too many to summarise here. But if you have maternity rights laid down in your contract, or if you are trying to negotiate a maternity scheme with your employers, the points to watch out for are these.

Qualifying period

The most generous maternity schemes demand no particular period of service before you qualify for job protection and other maternity rights. Teachers at some universities, for example, have full rights to paid leave from the moment they take up their jobs. There is no question here that you will lose out simply because you have not worked the required number of years or months.

Other employers, though less generous than this, still improve considerably on the standard legal rules. Some simply reduce the term of service to a year (for example, British Telecom, Atomic Energy Authority, British Airways) or eighteen months (for example, Containerlink). Others provide a shorter period of leave for those who have worked for less than two years. The NHS Whitley Council, for example, has agreed that women with just one year's service can take 18 weeks' paid leave. And those with under a year's service can take 18 weeks' unpaid leave.

The difficulties of a qualifying period can also be eased by reciprocal agreements which allow you to count work for a previous employer as part of your qualifying service. This is now quite common in the Civil Service and Local Government, where work in separate but similar departments can count as continuous employment with the same employer.

Length of maternity leave

Some maternity schemes offer more than the legal minimum of forty weeks' leave. The public sector is often the best in this respect. The Civil Service now gives up to 52 weeks' leave of absence. In the private sector, some of the most generous schemes are those negotiated by the National Union of Journalists. NUJ members at Penguin Books, for example, can take up to 52 weeks maternity leave after just one year of service. But *length* of maternity leave on its own is probably not the crucial factor for most working women. Few of us can afford to take much time off without pay. Leave is only *real leave* if it is paid.

Level of maternity pay

You will be looking ideally for a contract that goes beyond the legal minimum of six weeks at 90 per cent of full pay (before the lower rate of SMP starts – see pp. 31-4). The best will both give you a *longer period* of paid absence and keep you on *full salary*, rather than the reduced rate of 90 per cent. Like many schemes, the arrangement at Penguin Books incorporates a sliding scale of payment – with 20 weeks on full pay, 10 weeks on half pay and the remainder unpaid.

'Incentives' to go back to work

Many companies only offer their full maternity benefits to those who do actually return to work. And they may withhold part of your maternity pay until you have been fully back at work for a certain length of time. British Telecom, for example, offers thirteen weeks' leave at full pay after one year's service, but withholds the last five weeks of this until the woman has been back at work for 13 weeks. Other employers offer a 'bonus' if you return to work at all, or (more commonly) once you have been back for a specified period. This second arrangement is to prevent you coming back to work, collecting the bonus, then immediately resigning!

Flexibility of return

A few maternity schemes offer a flexible return to work (often part-time to start with) over a period of years. Most simply specify a maximum period of leave – and after that you either go back full-time, resign your job or take pot luck that your firm might have a part-time vacancy that would suit you. But it is a feature of some industries (particularly, but not only, the major banks) that they allow a complete 'career break' or a period of part-time work, before you return to full-time work. Barclays, Midland and National Westminster all operate this kind of scheme. Barclays, for example, allows women above a certain grade (those believed to have 'management potential') to take two years off after the end of their maternity leave – provided that they take on two weeks' 'relief work' for the bank each year. Alternatively they can work part-time for two years, before coming back to a full-time job.

Schemes of this type have had a lot of publicity. They do represent some of the most interesting developments in maternity arrangements. And they are spreading. Recently a large firm of solicitors in Bristol introduced a scheme for nine months' absence, plus nine months' part-time working; while the National Union of Teachers has negotiated a seven-year career break for its women members in Kent. Even so, they are still restricted to a few businesses – and often to only a few women within those businesses. They are not maternity *rights* for anyone.

Adoptive mothers

Some maternity schemes recognise the needs of adoptive mothers by providing a period of leave (usually unpaid) when the child is first brought home. These arrangements are normally much less generous than those that apply to natural mothers – for example, the London Borough of Lambeth's scheme, which gives an adoptive mother the option of six months' unpaid maternity leave, or leave until the child is a year old. But a few (such as, again, some schemes negotiated by the NUJ) offer adoptive mothers exactly the same (paid) rights as natural parents.

Fathers

Rather more employers now offer some form of paternity leave for husbands or partners. But very few offer more than ten days' paid absence around the time of the baby's birth. Typical are three days at the Automobile Association and five days for employees of the London Borough of Camden.

GETTING YOUR RIGHTS

Many employers are keen to get a fair deal for their women employees, pregnant or not – and they will go to some trouble to inform you of the rights you are entitled to over your maternity period. In my own case, the University administration rang me up just to check that I knew exactly how much paid leave I was allowed to take. I had decided for various reasons to go back to work two weeks before it was necessary – and they were worried that either I didn't know what my rights were or had been unfairly pressured by my colleagues to return to work early! But other employers are not so helpful. This is not always because they are determined to be uncooperative over maternity rights. Often they do not themselves fully understand the complicated regulations that govern maternity pay, leave and reinstatement.

There are several useful sources of advice if you think you are not getting your maternity rights. First you need to make sure what those rights are. Your local Social Security Office may be able to help. If not, you can get reliable information on the technicalities of the employment legislation from one of the regional offices of ACAS. Or, for advice on maternity pay and related social security benefits, call *Freeline Social Security* (0800 666555), a free phone service set up to deal with all general enquiries about benefits and National Insurance. Within your own organisation, your trade union representative should be able to help with establishing your rights and negotiating with your employers. If you are not a member of a Trade Union, you could try a local Citizens Advice Bureau or Neighbourhood Law Centre.

Most problems will be solved by discussing the matter with your employers or using the established 'grievance procedure' within your organisation. But if you find that you are still denied your rights, your only choice (apart from giving up!) is to go to an Industrial Tribunal. In the first instance the tribunal will send your case to a conciliation officer from ACAS, who will try to bring both sides together and arrange a negotiated settlement. If this fails, the tribunal will adjudicate between you and your employer according to the terms of the relevant Employment Act (and subsequent legal decisions). If it finds in your favour, your rights (to pay or job security) will be enforced or you will be offered compensation.

If you want to take a case to an Industrial Tribunal, you

should obtain form IT1 (or IT1 (Scot) in Scotland) from any Unemployment Benefit Office or Jobcentre. Don't delay. Complaints to tribunals should normally be made within three months of the grievance occurring. Industrial Tribunals are intended to be held in such a way that you can put your own case without having to engage expensive legal experts. Nevertheless, you would be well advised to get the help of your Trade Union or, at least, have an interview with a solicitor before embarking on your case. Many lawyers offer a 'fixed fee' interview (30 minutes' advice for a small fixed sum) or you may qualify for Legal Aid to have a solicitor help you *prepare your case* (but *not* – according to the rules for Legal Aid – to appear at the tribunal on your behalf).

A few cases concerned with maternity rights have been brought to an Industrial Tribunal under the Sex Discrimination Act, not the various employment laws. If you think this might be an option for you, you should get in touch with the Equal Opportunities Commission – as well as the people listed above. But remember that under the Sex Discrimination Act, even if you win your case, the tribunal has limited powers. It cannot, for example, insist on your reinstatement at work if you have been unfairly dismissed; it can only provide you with compensation.

*

In general, the best advice is *don't panic.* Even though the system of maternity benefits is quite needlessly complicated, most women who qualify do actually get their benefits. If you are reading this at the beginning of your pregnancy, you will probably feel that you will never master all the different dates and payments and rights. You will be amazed to find in a few weeks that you are talking about SMP and 'the eleventh week before the expected date of confinement' as if you had known about it all your life!

If you are one of the (many) unlucky ones who do not qualify for the major maternity rights, whether from the government or a private scheme, don't give up yet. Read the next few chapters and think about how you would manage

with a small baby and a full-time job. Then go to your
employers with a proposition – for unpaid leave, if necessary.
And don't take the first no for an answer. Remember, even if
your childcare seems cripplingly expensive and even if you
need several months' leave without pay, you will still be
better off *in the long run* than staying at home without a job.

3

How to cope: the bare essentials

It is not an easy life being a working mother. If you are very rich, of course, you will be able to give yourself a relatively untroubled time by hiring a regiment of nannies and domestic help. But this is not the case for most of us – who have to rush home from work, pick up the baby from the minder's, feed it, play with it, get it to bed, clear up the toys and do the washing-up, before we have any time to ourselves. Working mothers are quite simply 'over-employed'. Even if you have full-time childcare during your working hours, you are still looking after (and, hopefully, having fun with) your kids after work and at weekends, as well as coping with the usual household chores. One American survey revealed that mothers who had full-time work still spent an average of thirty-five hours a week on household jobs. Maybe you are more prepared to live with a bit of dirt than most American women. But, even so, to have a job and a family is a tough assignment.

This chapter looks at some of the basic rules of 'how to manage'. There are many varieties of childcare. But, whatever option you choose, some questions will remain the same. How will you feed him while you are at work? Will you be able to go on breast-feeding? How do you find the time to buy all the nappies, baby-wipes, and all the other baby essentials you seem to run out of every week? How do you get the washing and the cleaning done – and still have time to do something you want to do every now and then? There are no miracle answers – but there are some tips that will help you cope with, and even enjoy, the whole experience.

FOOD: MAINLY MILK

Bottles

If you are going back to work very soon after your baby is born, it may well be easiest to change to bottle-feeding. This is particularly true if you work long and irregular hours, and your baby is not to be cared for near your place of work. Don't get depressed by the 'breast-feeding' brigade! They mean well, but a lot of the propaganda is overstated. You will *not* be doing your baby irreparable harm if you switch to formula after a few weeks. You are, in fact, more likely to harm him by wearing *yourself* out in a desperate attempt to continue breast-feeding against all the odds. Besides, you will already have done your baby a great deal of good if you have fed him yourself for only a few weeks or even just a few days. For it is the colostrum (which he will get from you in the first days after the birth) that is *particularly* rich in antibodies to protect him from disease.

Bottle-feeding is easy to fit in with your childcare arrangements. You can mix up the feeds for the day yourself in the morning – and either leave them in the fridge for your nanny, or take them (in a cold bag) to the fridge at your childminder's or nursery. Alternatively you can just provide the powdered formula, and whoever looks after your baby can mix up the feed as it is needed. Both these schemes allow you total freedom from feeding during the day. You should never have to return to the baby unexpectedly simply because the food has run out. Even if you generally provide ready-mixed bottles, your child-carer should always have some extra formula to hand for use in an emergency.

For some working mothers bottle-feeding will be the only practical option. A busy lawyer, for example, who commutes fifty miles to work and sometimes has to stay late at the office, leaving her six-week-old baby with nanny or husband, will sensibly choose to give up breast-feeding. Many other women find that they can continue to feed the baby themselves, even if they fall back on formula from time to time. It is obviously easier if you return to work when your child is a little older (say five or six months) and has already started on a mixed diet. But it is not impossible to manage even with a tiny baby. There are various different arrangements that you could try.

Breast and bottle

One arrangement is to provide formula feeds for the baby by day, and to continue breast-feeding in the early mornings, evenings and at weekends. The advantages of this system are clear. You are completely free of any commitment to feeding the baby during the day – which is useful if you have a particularly busy schedule. But at night you can continue with the convenience and pleasure of breast-feeding, as well as feeling that the baby is getting the best possible food. Your milk-supply will naturally adjust itself, as the child sucks less and so gives less stimulus to your milk production. It sounds perfect, and some mothers manage to make it work. But there are problems.

You will need to prepare the baby *in advance* for sucking from a bottle. Don't send him off to the childminder one day with a bottle of milk under his arm and expect him to feed happily. Many breastfed babies are very reluctant at first to take milk from a bottle – and you will need some time to experiment, getting the right shaped teat, the right-sized hole and the most comfortable position. Different babies have different preferences. So don't give up if he refuses the first bottle you give him. Try a different teat. There are an enormous variety on the market.

Your problems may not be over once you have induced the baby to take formula from a bottle. Some babies, once they have learnt the art of sucking from a bottle, are reluctant to return to the breast – which is apparently rather more exhausting work! It is a good idea, at least to start with, not to feed the baby with a bottle yourself. Leave that to your partner or child-carer. If *you* never give him a bottle, the baby may associate the pleasure of being close to you directly with the breast – and so return to it happily after a day on a rubber teat. This separation between bottle- and breast-feeding may also help you manage the opposite problem. If you have found that the baby will not take a feed when *you* offer him the bottle, get your partner to try. It sometimes happens that the baby is only reluctant to suck from a bottle when he senses that he is being perversely deprived of the breast!

Breast-feeding: the routine of expressing

If you want your baby to keep to a diet of breast-milk, you may decide to express your own milk regularly (see pp. 49-54). You would then give this to your child-carer to feed to the baby, rather than formula. The organisation of this will be pretty complicated, but not unmanageable if you are determined to succeed. You will need to have a place at work where it is convenient to express your milk at least once a day, access to a fridge to store the milk in, preferably sterilising equipment, a cold box to transport it and a child-carer who is sympathetic to your plans and understands the general rules of hygiene for handling breast milk (see pp. 54-6). If you have all these, you should be able to get into a routine of producing milk at the office one day for your baby to drink the next. You cannot be *certain* that this will work for you. Some women do find expressing very difficult and time-consuming. But others have been known to keep a pair of hungry twins going in this way, regularly expressing large quantities of milk in their lunch break.

A routine of expressing will be almost impossible to establish if you have an irregular timetable (if, for example, you are often travelling) or if there is no place at your work where you can easily express. Once again, it really is better to opt for formula than to make your life a misery trying unsuccessfully to express enough to keep up with the baby. There is also not much point in trying if your nursery or child-minder is not happy with the system. You cannot risk making your baby ill because whoever is feeding him does not take the proper trouble in handling and preparing the milk, or is simply too busy to do so.

Occasional problems can still crop up, even if you do find that you and your child-carer easily get into the routine. You could have some initial difficulties getting the baby to take to the bottle. It may be breast-milk that he is drinking, but it is still coming from a rubber teat! So try the suggestions already made on pp. 46-7. From time to time accidents will happen – like not getting the chance to express enough one day or the fridge breaking down. To guard against this kind of thing, you must make sure that your child-carer has a back-up supply of formula that she can feed the baby, or some of your own milk (perhaps expressed before you returned to work) in her deep-freeze.

Breast-feeding: taking yourself to the baby

If you go back to work after your baby has become settled into a regular routine and if he is looked after at or near your place of work, you may be able to go on feeding him yourself, without bothering with a bottle. Suppose he is feeding regularly every four hours. You could feed him at 9 o'clock, just before you leave for work or immediately you arrive at the nursery or minder's. You could then come back again to feed him at lunch-time – and be with him shortly after 5 for another feed. *In principle* he need never have to deal with a rubber teat.

This is a very high-risk way of organising your life. It isn't really worth attempting unless you have some flexibility at your place of work. You must be at the end of a telephone and generally be able to drop everything and go to the baby if he gets hungry sooner than you expected. You will also need the *wholehearted* cooperation of whoever looks after your child – because it is all too easy for your child-carer (consciously or unconsciously) to make the whole arrangement unworkable.

Imagine you have left your baby at his nursery and plan to return to feed him at 1 o'clock. At 12.30 he wakes up screaming for food. The care assistant rings you at work but your line is engaged. She has two other babies who need attention – so she gets a bottle of juice for yours and he eagerly drinks a good half. You turn up at one to feed him, but he is so full of orange that he takes only half his usual feed. At 3 o'clock (when you are in the middle of an important meeting) he is screaming for food again. And so on... The attitudes of the nursery staff are understandable. What would *you* do in their position? Half an hour with a screaming baby and other things to do is a *very* long time. But, from your point of view, you will only be able to work this system successfully if *they* make it a priority to save the baby's hunger for you and only give him the absolute minimum extra food and drink. It is probably easier with your own nanny at home. After all, she does not usually have other tiny babies to care for – and, if need be, she can devote all her energies to distracting yours from his hunger pangs.

Some working mothers really do manage always to be there at the right time, and their babies never even see a bottle. Most of us are not so efficient or have more complicated lives. You will need to think ahead about how your child-carer is going to cope on those occasions when you simply cannot be there to feed. You should leave a quantity of formula with her or, if you prefer, expressed milk – either chilled or frozen. And remember it would be kind to your child-carer to give your baby a bit of practice on a bottle, before expecting her to get eight ounces of formula down a screaming baby who has never sucked on anything but a breast!

The mechanics of expressing

There are three ways of expressing milk from your breasts – by electric pump, manual pump or by hand. There are advantages and disadvantages in each. But all will make you feel somewhat like a cow! The whole enterprise *is* faintly ridiculous – but still often more convenient than making up all those bottles of formula.

Electric pumps

These are by far the most efficient way of expressing large

Types of breast pump

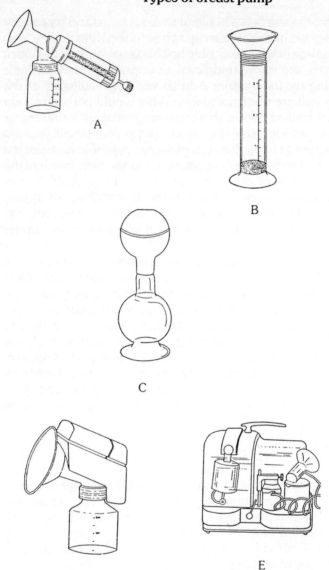

A, B – syringe-type manual pumps; C – motor-horn-type manual pump;
D – battery-operated electric pump; E – large electric pump.
Not to scale!

quantities of milk. A plastic funnel fits over your breast and the suction action of the pump draws the milk off into a bottle. Most of the pumps available are quite bulky and expensive. They are several pounds in weight and can cost quite a lot more than most standard pieces of household equipment – washing machines, freezers etc. As you are unlikely to want such an object as a permanent possession, it is easiest and cheaper to hire one from the NCT, the La Leche League (an organisation to promote breast-feeding) or directly from some manufacturers. But even so the cost mounts up if you need to have one over a period of months.

If it is very important to you to have something smaller and lighter, there are now some electric mini-pumps available. They sell for about a tenth of the price of a big model, and so may be a reasonable proposition to buy. But remember, they will be less efficient at pumping than the bigger, more powerful versions. And people do complain that they are *constantly* having to buy new batteries for them.

Very few women have any difficulty in expressing milk with an electric pump and you should manage to empty your breasts in about fifteen minutes or so. Read the instructions that come with the pump very carefully and go slowly when you first start – the amount of suction that some of the pumps can generate may be a bit of a shock! If you have trouble getting started, it helps to stroke your breast as you pump and actually to think about your baby (not about the next lot of typing). But your problems are more likely to be problems of organisation. The big electric pumps are really too large to carry to and from work. So if your main time for expressing is midday, you will have to keep your pump at the office and express by hand, or by manual pump, when you are at home.

Manual pumps

These are small, cheap and light. For some women they are a great success – but many find that they work no better for drawing off milk than simply expressing by hand. They all have a small funnel to fit over your breast and a reservoir or bottle attached to catch the milk. The basic principle is that you set up a small vacuum in front of the breast, which draws out the milk from the nipple. This vacuum is created either by squeezing a rubber bulb at the end of the pump (in a contraption that looks like an old-fashioned motor-horn) or by slowly pulling out of the pump a close-fitting inner cylinder (as in a medical syringe).

It is much more difficult to get the flow of milk started with a manual pump. Again, thinking about your baby and stroking the breast can help. You could also try putting a warm flannel over the breast, or systematically massaging it – working from the top down and round towards the nipple. But you might still have trouble producing a steady flow and it can take (literally) hours to collect less than half a single feed for a hungry baby. In this case it would obviously be a useless method for regular expressing at work. If, on the other hand, you can get the manual pumps to work well – then you have an almost ideal system for expressing milk which doesn't need any compli-cated machinery.

The best advice is to give these pumps a try. They are so cheap that you have little to lose. But don't be disappointed if you cannot manage to produce more than a couple of ounces of milk. You can always move on to an electric pump, if you need to express regular large amounts. Or you might even find that you get on better expressing by hand.

Hand expressing

Expressing by hand is probably easier than you would imagine. Do not be put off by those instruction manuals which seem to turn it into a high art form – with baffling diagrams of the internal construction of the breast and precise rules about where you should or should not apply pressure. The basic principles are quite straightforward and you will need to find out by trial and error whether you can get it to work for you. Some people are never successful, beyond a few tiny drops to mix with the baby's first rice cereal. Others will find it at least as easy as a manual pump.

In order to get a reasonable quantity of milk out of your breasts you have to press not the nipple itself, but the milk reservoirs that lie behind it. Try it this way.

- First of all stroke or massage your breasts for a few minutes, starting from the top and working down and round towards the nipple. This is to stimulate the milk-flow from the milk producing cells deep in the breast to the reservoirs near the surface.
- Then, choose whichever side seems most comfortable and, if you like, support your breast with one hand. With the other, place your thumb and forefingers on either edge of the dark area of the nipple. The best position for the thumb and fingers varies a little from person to person – but it will most likely be just inside or just outside the dark area.
- Then squeeze your thumb and fingers together, at the same time pushing slightly inwards towards your chest – and the milk should come!

If the milk doesn't come, don't give up. Alter the position of your fingers a little and also the direction of your squeezing. If it still doesn't work, keep calm, think about your baby, stroke your breast again – then have another go, as long as it is not hurting you. (If it is, stop!) You will know that you have got it right when the milk comes out not in tiny drops, but in several little jets.

The best place for your first attempts is probably the bath. The nice warm environment may help the milk flow (as will a warm wet flannel over your breasts). And you can squirt happily into the water, without having to bother about collecting the milk. When you have got the technique mastered, of course, you will need to catch the milk in something. Any old bowl will do (provided it is sterile – see pp. 54-5). But it is actually useful (and encouraging) to know exactly *how much* you are managing to express as you go along. I ended up hand-expressing into a manual pump! The pump (the syringe type) had a wide funnel, and a bottle, marked in ounces, screwed directly onto it. I squirted my milk into the funnel – and, as it dripped through into the bottle, I could keep track of how many ounces I had produced.

Don't be over-optimistic about how much milk you will manage to express. If you choose to do it in the morning (when the milk is most plentiful) and if you keep at it for half an hour or so (alternating from breast to breast, a few minutes on each) – then you can be reasonably pleased with yourself if you end up with three ounces of milk.

Don't become fixated on emptying your breasts *completely* as some books imply that you should. You won't have the time to do this by hand – and, in any case, you will never manage it. The breasts go on producing continuously, so that there are *always* a few drops left. Never bother to go on expressing once the milk has ceased to come in jets.

Hand-expressing is not the method to use if you depend on producing large quantities of milk regularly and quickly. But if you manage it reasonably well, it may be the simplest way of building up a stand-by reserve of milk in your freezer. I found that I easily got into the routine of expressing just two ounces of milk a day. My baby was never ravenously hungry in the morning and I could quickly express that small amount before giving him his breakfast-time feed and letting him finish off the still large quantity that was left. In only four days, I would have in store enough for a generous eight-ounce feed.

Handling, transporting and freezing breast milk

Breast milk provides a happy breeding ground for bacteria. The main rule for safe expressing is to keep everything as clean as possible – and mostly *sterile*. When you express, follow these guidelines:

- Always wash your hands before handling your pump or starting to express.
- If you are at home, immediately before you express sterilise the bottle in which the milk will be collected or stored, and the parts of the pump through which the milk will pass (these will be easily detachable from the pump).
- If you use sterilising tablets or special sterilising fluid, rinse everything in boiled water before actually using it.
- If you are expressing at work, sterilise the bottle and the

parts of the pump at home. Take them to work, preferably in a sterile paper bag – the sort used in hospitals, which you can get from big chemists or medical suppliers.

Useful for storing and transporting the milk are the disposable plastic bags that come (instead of a bottle) with the Playtex feeding system (available at many chemists). These are ready sterilised – so you can store milk in them (clipping the top with a metal tie) without the need for boiling water or for sterilising tablets. And they take up very little room in the freezer.

If you intend to use the milk within the next forty-eight hours, you need only keep it *chilled* until you are ready to warm it for use. Put it into a refrigerator straight away and when you transport it make sure that it stays cold. Either use a cold-box with ice packs in, or put it (in a Playtex plastic bag) into a wide-necked vacuum flask with some ice blocks. Whichever method you use for carrying the milk around, you always should check that the milk still does feel really cold when you take it out. *Never* let it stand at room temperature.

If you want to freeze your milk in a deep freeze, the procedure is a little more complicated. But it is worth it, just to build a reserve supply of breast milk. The process of freezing will destroy some of the antibodies in the milk. But don't worry about this. Your baby is not being fed *solely* on frozen milk – and if he was having formula, he wouldn't be getting any antibodies anyway! Remember these simple rules and you should have no trouble:

- You must keep milk at really low temperatures (below zero degrees Fahrenheit). That means a proper freezer, not the ice-box compartment of an ordinary refrigerator.
- You should get your milk into the freezer as soon as possible after you have expressed it. If you are expressing at work, then keep it chilled until you can get it frozen at home.
- Don't use glass containers to freeze the milk. They may crack at low temperatures. Put it into either sterile plastic bottles or ready-sterilised plastic bags.

- Label the milk with the date, so that you are sure to use the oldest first.
- Note the amount in each container. When you are making up a complete feed you will need to know how much you have in each little bottle or bag.
- Don't use frozen milk if it is older than six months.
- Thaw frozen milk under the tap. Run cold water on the bottle or bag first, then gradually change to warm water.
- Once the milk is liquid, either keep it chilled in the fridge for up to three hours. Or prepare it straight away for the baby, heating it to the required temperature in a bowl of hot water or in a saucepan of water on the cooker.
- Never leave the frozen milk to thaw by itself in the open air.
- Never heat it from frozen on the cooker.
- Never *refreeze* any breast milk that has thawed. Be particularly careful if you want to add fresh milk to a container of already frozen milk. Don't add the new milk while it is still warm – for it would slightly melt the top layer of the frozen milk, which would then *refreeze*. Chill the new milk for a short while, and then add it to the frozen container.

Help

Expressing milk can seem almost effortless when you get into the swing. But at the beginning you may feel that you will never produce more than a few feeble drops in a saucer. If you think you are not getting anywhere, contact your local NCT breastfeeding counsellor (see National Childbirth Trust in your phone book) or a local group of the La Leche League. They will be able to give you more *practical* help and advice than any book. And, remember, the problems will not last long. Even if you *now* feel worn down by the bottles, the pumps, the sterilisers, the milk-stained T-shirts – in a year's time you may feel quite nostalgic for that early period of closeness between you and the baby.

WEANING FOODS

Before long your child will be tucking into healthy (or not so healthy) meals. You will have forgotten all your worries about breast pumps or formula. Instead, you will be trying to work out how to get the little darling to eat fewer chips, less coke, more apples and wholemeal bread. But between the milk and the chips comes a strange period of 'weaning foods' – a range of various kinds of 'mush', which gradually gets the infant taste and digestive system used to a grown-up diet. How does the working mother cope with this stuff?

Ready-prepared food

Don't be too strict with yourself. Don't reject those little commercial jars out of hand. Many are quite good nutritionally. And there are bound to be times when they are absolute life-savers – when you are out in the car or when you have not had time to prepare anything else. But be careful!

- Scrutinise the ingredients on the side of the jar very closely – unless you are very keen on feeding your six-month-old loads of sugar. *You* may never have thought of adding sugar to 'savoury beef dinner', but you can be certain that this precisely what most baby food manufacturers will do. And the sugar is likely to masquerade on the label under a variety of different (technical) disguises – 'dextrose', 'sucrose' or 'maltodextrin' (not in fact sugar, but still a sweetener). You can take it as a general rule that unless the jar or packet explicitly says 'no added sugar', sugar will be there. And even 'no added sugar', can still mean that maltodextrin is there.
- Taste the commercial baby-foods that you think of offering to your child. Some will be really quite nice. But others will be dreadfully sweet. And others still will be dreary and bland – tasting more of the cornflour (added for cheap padding) than of the fresh English fruits pictured on the outside. Ask yourself if you want this kind of sludge to be your baby's introduction to the pleasures of eating.

It is depressing to think of most of your baby's diet being a combination of sugar and flour. So what are the alternatives to commercial jars, if you are not going to spend hours straining fruit through a sieve?

Natural and home-made foods

Some natural foods come almost ready prepared. It is no trouble to mash up a banana or an avocado, for example. And you can easily take any soft fruit round to your childminder for your baby to eat at lunchtime. But for a wider range of tastes and nutrition, you will need to think ahead and (once again) make use of your freezer.

One of the best early foods, which you can give to a baby as young as four months, is puréed pear. There is no need to commit yourself (and your probably reluctant child-carer) to cooking one pear on its own every time and then pushing it through a sieve. That would probably take almost twenty minutes altogether – and those twenty minutes could be much better spent. Instead, buy a couple of pounds of good fresh eating pears and stew them gently in a very little water until they are just soft enough to purée. Put them through a sieve or (quicker) in the blender until they are the right consistency – then transfer the mixture into ice-cube trays and put them in the freezer. When you need a portion for a tiny baby, just press out one cube from the tray. As he gets bigger, he may eat two or three – but the tray will still contain enough for ten or so meals.

You don't have to stop at puréed pears. You can make up trays of other kinds of fruit, of puréed fish or meat, as well as mashed vegetables. And eventually you can move on to toddler-sized pots of soups, home-made baked beans and casseroles. Freezing does remove a little of the nutritional value of the food. But it is only a little. And the other advantages of preparing food in this way are tremendous. You can get a lot ready in a short time. You know what is in it (or rather what is not). And it actually tastes like 'real food'!

You will need to be careful over hygiene when you are preparing frozen food like this for a very young child. But

bacteria do not breed so fast in other foods as they do in milk
– so the rules are not quite so strict:

- Wash your hands and the cooking utensils carefully before
  you start and sterilise the ice-tray (if your baby is still very
  young).
- Put the food straight into the freezer as soon as it is cool.
  Don't ever let it stand around.
- Use the frozen food within six weeks.
- When you remove it from the freezer, let the food thaw
  gradually (either in the refrigerator or at room temperature)
  and make sure that it is thoroughly defrosted before you
  feed it to the baby.
- If the meal contains frozen fish or meat, *boil* it after it has
  thawed and immediately before you use it.
- Never refreeze the food once it has defrosted.

For a working mother a freezer is second only to a washing
machine in the list of essential equipment. From breast-milk
to baked beans, you can always keep something in it that
your child can eat. And you can fill it up at times that suit *you*
– when you have got the baby off to bed or when you just
happen to feel like cooking. Not only that – you can reserve a
small corner for treats for yourself. There are bound to be
some nights when a ready-made meal from the freezer is all
that you will have the energy to cook!

MAKING LIFE EASIER

Working mothers should put a high priority on making sure
they *enjoy* the time they have with their children. Saturdays
can be hell – struggling back from the shops, bags over each
arm, boxes of nappies balanced on the back of the buggy and a
screaming toddler writhing about in the seat. You mustn't let
this happen. Otherwise, by the time the kids have grown up, all
you will remember will be the exhaustion and inconvenience!
Everyone's life is different, and everyone has different ways of
making things easier for themselves. But here are some basic
guidelines that should apply to most people.

Nappies

Don't use terry nappies, unless you really cannot afford the disposable kind. Any working mother who willingly chooses nappies that need washing and sterilising deserves no sympathy. Even if you have a nanny at home who is prepared to handle the whole business during the week, you still have the weekends, the holidays and the times when she is ill. Don't add to your burdens – use disposables. They *are* expensive. An average baby will use up most of his Child Benefit in nappies. But it is worth every penny – and you will feel relatively rich again once you have got the kids potty-trained!

Supplies

Get supplies delivered to your door. Lots of firms offer free delivery of nappies, if you order in large quantities. And you can get other kinds of baby-goods (nappy-wipes, creams, shampoo, clothes) by mail order or even delivered by a local department store, if you have a charge account with them. In fact, some of the best modern designs for children's clothes are produced by mail-order companies.

If you have a nanny, you might think that she could buy all this kind of thing during her working hours. Of course, she could – and it will probably be convenient for her to buy many of the smaller items and clothes. But do you really want her to spend her day heaving nappy boxes back from the shops, when she could be doing many more interesting things with the baby?

The nanny certainly won't want to spend her time shopping for goods for *you*, particularly your basic food supplies. Here too home deliveries can be a life saver. Many milkmen will now bring soft drinks, bread, cereals and a range of other food, if you order it in advance. And you will probably be suprised how many butchers and greengrocers in your area still offer a delivery service – even if they do not advertise it.

If you are going to use delivery services, you will have to make sure that someone is usually at home – or that there is somewhere else (perhaps a neighbour's) where the goods can be left. The only other alternative is that you get the deliveries sent to your workplace. If you usually *drive* to work, it is then quite simple to load up the car from your office and take the stuff straight home – certainly easier than doing the rounds of the shops. Of course, some of your colleagues may cast a wry smile when they see four giant boxes of nappies waiting at the reception. But who really cares about that?

Help

Pay for as much help in the house as you can possibly afford. Apart from a reliable washing machine and a freezer, money is better spent on people to help than on super new appliances. Suppose you do buy the latest new model super-suck vacuum cleaner. You still have to go round the house actually doing the cleaning yourself. Much better to stick with your old, bashed-up hoover – and have someone else do it for you. There is no need to think just in terms of an old fashioned 'Mrs Mop'. Some people get their parents to help out. Others find that sixth-formers eager to earn a few extra pounds a week make the most helpful and efficient cleaners of all!

Travelling

When you are travelling with the children, give yourself as much comfort as possible. It is important not to become a hermit – buried at work during the week and at home during the weekend. You *must* get out to see your friends and take weekends away. Travelling by car is the ideal way to do it. You can stop for a break when you want and the children's seatbelts will at least keep them in one spot! But if you have to use public transport, how do you survive – and not arrive at the other end in such a state that you only wish that you had stayed at home?

Avoid buses. They only rarely have loos and there is hardly any space for a toddler to run around. Under almost any circumstances take the train. And if you can, travel first class.

This may seem ridiculously extravagant. But you will find that the extra space and the absence of fellow travellers will help your sanity no end. And remember that British Rail now has so many special fare offers that you can sometimes travel first class for only a pound or so more than the standard fare. Our family made several happy journeys on a Sunday between London and Cambridge, while the toddler played hide-and-seek in a completely empty first-class carriage. And with the weekend fare it all cost lest than an ordinary second-class ticket! But be warned – if you find fellow travellers in the first class, they are not likely to be friendly. Most people, after all, pay the extra fare precisely so that they can *avoid* having to sit with sticky, boisterous little girls!

Escape

The final secret behind an easier life is to escape from the children now and then. If you can arrange some weekends away on your own, so much the better. But don't forget the evenings. Don't try to make up for being away all day by having your toddler under your feet until midnight. You need some time for yourself, for your partner and for your friends without the children. Make it a priority to get them to bed at a reasonable time. And don't be squeamish about leaving them to cry a bit, if it is the only way you can get them into a routine. You want to enjoy your children – but that partly depends on having a good *adult* life too.

Taking the baby to work

You may be tempted in some jobs to take your baby to work with you. Sometimes this will be inevitable. Your childcare arrangements may have broken down, or you may simply not be able to afford to have your baby looked after all the hours you need to be at work – especially if you have to be on call or attend meetings at unpredictable times. But, as a general rule, *leave the children behind*. And at all costs avoid the macho-motherhood, my-baby's-been-to-more-meetings-than-he's-had-hot-dinners syndrome!

Workplaces are no fun for babies. Young children are quite unsuited to places where they are not allowed to make a noise – or where they can't crawl around and undo every shoelace in the room. Besides, they are a dreadful disruption for everyone else. *You* may think that your baby will be no bother. You will put him in his carrycot and leave him behind your chair at the meeting. If he cries, you will pick him up – otherwise he will just gurgle happily. To *you* he is the most charming thing in the world, and could never cause offence. You forget that to the rest of your colleagues he is just another, quite ordinary, messy infant. And, like all infants, he is either making a dreadful noise at this very minute – or, if not, then he is just about to. That charming gurgle is just a portent of a horrid wail to come.

Babies *are* distracting and disruptive. And they are a positive aggravation to other working mothers among your colleagues, who have probably gone to a lot of trouble and expense to get *their* kids looked after. Never mix business and babies, unless it is a crisis – or unless you are trying to make some political point about the unavailability of childcare!

4

Nannies: their training and qualifications

Once upon a time only the very rich had nannies. They lived in nursery wings in great houses, wore uniforms with frilly hats and took their charges to the park in large 'battle-ship' prams. The best sort of all never married. They stayed with their family for generation after generation – surviving (at least in the story books) to pin the nappies of the grandchildren of their first charges! No doubt these ladies do still exist, somewhere. But most nannies are now a very different breed. And they are employed by families who are far from aristocratic.

There are now more nannies working in private families than ever before. In many ways this is a sad state of affairs. Often girls have gone into this kind of work without any training whatsoever, simply because they cannot find any other job. It is the modern equivalent of 'entering service' – as those from the unemployed North seek domestic work in the prosperous South. And even the great expansion of proper nursery nurse training schemes in the 1970s has gone somewhat awry. This expansion went hand in hand with optimistic plans to increase the number of pre-school nursery places. More nannies were needed, it was thought, to meet the demand for qualified child-carers in the new, state-run, nursery schools. But only a few of those new nursery schools ever materialised. And many of the girls who enter childcare courses find that (like it or not) the only jobs they can get are on the private nanny market.

From the employer's point of view, of course, this is all good news. The competition to get a really *first-rate* nanny may be intense – there are never enough to go round! But there is, in general, a plentiful supply of people looking for this kind of work, and newly-trained girls are coming out of the colleges each year. And you no longer have to be incredibly rich to afford a nanny. It is still the most expensive form of childcare, if you have only one child. But if you have two or more young children, a nanny may be cheaper than sending them to a good private day nursery. The reason for this is quite simply that nursery nursing, like most female 'caring' professions, is badly paid. It may *seem* a lot to you, when you are trying to find the nanny's salary out of your own income – and still have some left over. After all, you might be badly paid too. But no ordinary nanny gets rich on her weekly wage.

This chapter, and the next, look at the formal side of employing a nanny. Here I shall deal with the qualifications a nanny may have. What does it mean when she says she is an 'NNEB', is 'Norland trained' or has an 'NAMCW certificate'? What is the difference between a 'nanny' and a 'mother's help'? Chapter 5 looks at the obligations you have as a nanny's employer – and how you cope with them. How do you draw up a nanny's terms of employment when she begins the job? How do you deal with her tax and National Insurance contributions? What are her rights if you decide to fire her? Of course, you will have to think about many other things if you are to find a good nanny and keep her (see Chapters 6 and 7). If you want some idea of what it is like living and working with a nanny, go straight to Chapter 7. But this chapter and the next give you the basic reference information you need to know before you think of employing anyone.

COURSES AND QUALIFICATIONS

Nannies may have a bewildering range of qualifications. You probably will not have heard of most of them. And you will have still less of an idea what they might *mean*. Up to a point this does not matter. If you like the person you employ, if you can trust her and if she is good with your child, then you are not going to bother whether she is an 'NNEB' or a 'BTEC'. But many girls will certainly turn up at their interview flourishing a range of impressive-looking certificates. So it really is worth knowing what it all amounts to – what level the qualifications are, and what skills they have been taught. As a basic rule, the more impressive the certificate, the less worthwhile the qualification! But there is a bit more to it than that.

National Nursery Examination Board

The certificate of the National Nursery Examination Board is the main qualification for childcare of the very young. The course leading to this certificate normally lasts two years and is available at about 150 technical colleges and colleges of further education throughout the country, training over 5,000 students a year. There are no national entry requirements for the course, but many colleges ask for at least two or three GCSEs (at grades A to C – the old O-level standard). Most people start the course at sixteen, but it is possible to enter later or as a 'mature student'. Almost all the students are female, but boys are welcome on most courses and some do go on to become nursery nurses and nannies.

The course offers a training in all aspects of the care of children between birth and the age of seven. It is divided into classroom theory and practical work on 'placements' in nursery and infant schools, hospitals and private families. The details and the time spent on each area vary a little from college to college. But a common arrangement is for three days a week to be spent in the classroom and two on placement.

The certificate is awarded on the basis of two written papers taken at the end of the course (a multiple choice and an essay paper), and by continuous assessment both of written work and of the practical experience on the placements. A particular feature of the course is the 'child observations' in which students produce written reports on the behaviour and development of children they have met on their placements.

These range from accounts of how a handicapped baby manages with breast-feeding to interpretations of how a group of five-year-olds reacted to their first day at school. A file of between fifty and sixty of these observations forms part of the final course assessment.

An NNEB certificate does not *guarantee* a good nanny. Some girls scrape through the qualification with very little flair. Others may be talented, but only go into private nannying as very much second best. None of these are likely to be ideal. But the NNEB *does* ensure a basic level of competence. At the very least, an NNEB nanny will know how to change a nappy and should recognise a fever when she sees it. At the best, she will be a skilled and sympathetic child-carer, with a good idea of how to cope with any problem – from bee-stings to grandparents. And she will be more knowledgeable than you are ever likely to be on the finer points of child development!

A few private nannies may have taken the 'advanced NNEB' course – the CPQS (Certificate in Post Qualifying Studies). This is open to holders of the standard certificate (or other equivalent qualification) who have had at least two years full-time experience in childcare since leaving college. It takes the normal NNEB course on to roughly first-year University level, and offers a wide range of training in (for example) managerial skills, multi-cultural education, and the care of children with special needs, such as the terminally ill. It is an excellent course. But it is mostly followed by nursery nurses in institutions (schools or hospitals), who can get funding from their employers to attend.

Chiltern, Norland and Princess Christian

The closest you can now get to the 'traditional nanny' are girls trained at the Chiltern Nursery Training College, the Norland Nursery Training College and the Princess Christian College. These are all private residential colleges which prepare students for the NNEB certificate and (at the same time) for the Royal Society of Health Diploma in Nursery Nursing. This diploma covers very much the same ground as the NNEB, but candidates must be at least twenty years old and already have passed the NNEB exam. As with the usual NNEB training, the courses last for two years. But students at the private colleges do not begin until they are eighteen.

The main difference between one of these nannies and an NNEB from the local 'tech' is social. Most of the girls attending the private colleges are themselves well-heeled. The fees are hefty and Local Authority grants are only rarely available. The training offered is also towards a more upmarket *style* of nannying. Each of the colleges has its own particular uniform of a rather old-fashioned kind and they put more emphasis in their syllabus on such old-fashioned skills as needlework. The students too often learn to expect some of the trappings of the traditional nanny – not just the large pram, but even a nursery suite! They may also expect higher pay than the normal nanny, sometimes considerably higher.

The mystique surrounding the nannies from these colleges is not wholly justified. Their main qualification – the NNEB – is just the same as that of other nannies. And they do not need to meet higher *academic* standards to get in. All three colleges ask for just three GCSEs (grade C or above), like several of the Local Authority courses. That said, these residential colleges do offer some kinds of facilities and training not normally available elsewhere. All have their own day nursery attached to the college (and the Norland also has a residential nursery) where the students can get on-the-spot practical teaching. And the Chiltern arranges for its students to spend up to eight weeks resident at a maternity hospital – so that they can get plenty of experience of very tiny babies.

Montessori nannies

Another independent college offering training for the NNEB certificate is the London Montessori Centre. Here NNEB students also take the Montessori Child Care and Teaching Diploma. This introduces them to the philosophy and practice of the so-called 'Montessori method' of education, developed earlier this century by Maria Montessori. The method puts great emphasis on providing a 'prepared environment' in which children can learn 'naturally' – encouraged to absorb experiences and ideas at their own pace and to learn *self*-discipline, as well as independence and respect for others. The teacher is supposed to act as a *guide* to the child, not as an *instructor*. Montessori teachers have traditionally been associated with nursery and preparatory schools, but a few may become private nannies.

BTEC National Diploma in Nursery Nursing

The Business and Technician Education Council have recently sponsored this new qualification in nursery nursing, already available in a few technical colleges. The entry requirements are slightly higher than for most NNEB courses – four GCSEs at grade C or above. But from the employer's point of view there is probably not much to choose between this and the standard NNEB. For the nanny, on the other hand, there may be definite career advantages in taking the BTEC rather than the NNEB. The BTEC has been devised not only to provide a nursery nursing qualification, but also to be a recognised qualification for further courses in teaching (BEd) or the social services. After a few years as a nanny, many women want to move on into other areas – such as qualified infant teaching. With only an NNEB they have normally found that they have to return to college to get A-levels before starting a new course. The BTEC (it is hoped) will become widely accepted as the equivalent of A-levels.

City and Guilds and National Association of Maternal and Child Welfare (NAMCW)

These courses are not professional qualifications in nursery nursing. They include childcare, but as part of a broader area of study.

The City and Guilds Institute offers a variety of certificates, at many different levels. The one you are most likely to come across is the Certificate in Family and Community Care, which (as its title suggests) includes community work in youth clubs, schools and residential homes, as well as baby and childcare. The emphasis is more on practical than theoretical skills. And most colleges offering the course (which normally lasts two years) do not demand any particular exam qualifications for entry – or only the lowest grades at GCSE.

The NAMCW certificates also normally form part of general childcare courses, below the level of the NNEB. Many technical colleges run these courses over one or two years. They end up with a couple of GCSE exams (in English, Human Development, Psychology, etc), as well as these certificates in Childcare and others in Housecraft, First Aid and the like. Most of the people on these courses will not have been qualified for (or will have failed to get onto) an NNEB course.

You may find a really good nanny who has one of these certificates, rather than an NNEB. City and Guilds in particular attracts quite a lot of mature students, who have decided they want a 'caring job', rather than the office work they started on. But remember – however impressive the certificates may look, the qualifications are not the same as an NNEB.

'Experienced' nannies

In the world of nannying the phrase 'NNEB or experience' has a more precise meaning than you might think. It is generally thought that about three years' practical experience as a nanny (or, at first, as a 'mother's help', see opposite) is roughly equivalent to the two years' NNEB training. Some of the best nannies certainly have had no formal teaching in childcare. Instead, they have a natural flair with children and have learnt the basic rules 'on the job' (often having had younger brothers and sisters at home). Some will also have done a lot of reading on their own, which will more than make up for the theoretical part of the NNEB course. But unlike the NNEB nanny, you get no *guarantee* of a minimum level of competence with the 'experienced' girl. After all, the experience might have been a disaster – or, if not a disaster, then it might have been experience with a very different kind of family from yours, with a very different attitude to childcare. You will rely (perhaps too much for comfort) on the attitudes of her previous employers and the honesty of their references.

Mother's helps and au pairs

For full-time working mothers of very young children, neither mother's helps nor au pairs are a sensible option for childcare. A mother's help is an 'experienced' nanny without the experience! As the name implies, she works *with* a mother – normally doing some housework, as well as taking her share looking after the kids. She may sometimes have sole charge of them, but she is normally supervised. Most mother's helps have just left school. They are not childcare professionals. They are likely to be no better or worse than your average teenage babysitter – and you are almost certainly not going to be happy leaving them in charge of your baby all day while you are out at work and out of reach. In time, of course, things change. And some will gain enough on-the-job experience to count as an 'experienced' nanny. The half-way stage (perhaps just one or two years' experience) is often indicated as 'nanny/mothers help'. You may want to consider a girl at this stage for sole charge, if she is highly recommended and (more important) if you *feel* that she will cope.

The employment of au pairs is regulated by law. They are, strictly speaking, girls from western Europe aged between seventeen and twenty-seven. And the main purpose of their visit to the UK is to learn English (for which they normally attend a regular course). They are expected to do some housework and baby-sitting for *up to five hours a day* – and receive free accommodation and 'pocket money' in return. The limit on their hours of work puts them totally out of the question as childcarers for a full-time working mother. But even if you were working only part-time, an au pair would not be suitable to look after very young children. However intelligent (they are often, for example, pre-university students), they are likely to be quite untrained in childcare. And if they cannot speak English perfectly, they will find it very hard to cope in an emergency (if, for example, they have to deal with a doctor or hospital casualty department). Au pairs do not really come into their own until you have school-age children, when their hours can fit very well with picking up the kids from school and entertaining them till you get home.

Foreign girls who are employed longer hours than the maximum of five hours a day (up to thirty hours a week) are sometimes, euphemistically, known as 'au pairs plus'. In fact this category is not recognised by the Home Office employment regulations. They should be treated as formally 'employed' – not just given tax-free 'pocket money'. In most cases these girls have all the disadvantages of the untrained mother's help. And, in addition, they may have only a limited command of English. They are not a practical proposition for the full-time care of very small children – although (like au pairs) they may be a good bet for school-age kids.

*

Formal qualifications are not necessary for being a nanny. Some people really do find completely untrained girls who turn out to be brilliant at the job in every way. But don't be too romantic about 'natural gifts' in childcare. Looking after children is a career than demands commitment and patience. It's not all happy play and love and affection! If you have a trained nanny who has done a two-year course, you have some evidence of that commitment. And she will probably have a more realistic idea of the less glamorous side of the job – temper tantrums and endless nappies and wet knickers.

5

Nannies: the formalities of employment

For most people a nanny is their first (official) employee. So they have never before dealt with all the obligations of being an employer. This does not just involve calculating and paying tax and National Insurance contributions – though that is an important part. There are other basic rules of employment that everyone should follow. These range from a legal requirement that employers provide a brief written statement of the main terms and conditions of their employee's job – to a requirement that they follow a particular procedure if they wish to dismiss someone.

   This chapter summarises the main obligations you will have when you start to employ a nanny. It doesn't make particularly light reading. Employment law (like maternity legislation) rarely does. If you have not yet decided whether or not to have a nanny, it is probably best just to skim over the information quickly – so you know what will be involved if you *do* decide to employ someone yourself. Then come back to it later, if you actually need the information.

   Do remember – the rules may all *look* terribly complicated. But very many people manage to employ a nanny without any difficulty. However baffling the tax forms may seem at first, after a few weeks you will think of them as a normal part of life.

TAX AND NATIONAL INSURANCE

It is vitally important that you pay your nanny's tax and

National Insurance contributions. If you do not, you yourself could become liable for a large bill for back-tax, as well as a hefty fine. And your employee may lose her entitlement to a range of social security benefits, such as unemployment pay and retirement pensions. Remember – in law it is *your* responsibility to pay tax and National Insurance contributions for your employee, even though you may deduct some of those contributions from her wages. It is *you* that the Inland Revenue will be after, if they discover that you have been employing your nanny 'unofficially'.

It may seem a daunting prospect to deal with the bureaucracy of the Inland Revenue, to work out from scratch how much you have to deduct from the nanny's wages each week and then to send it off to the right government department. If you already have an accountant, he or she will probably be prepared to do it all for you. You just tell him what you want to pay the nanny – and he will tell you exactly what you deduct, and what you you send to the taxman, and when. He will charge you for this service, of course – but you may think the expense worth it, just to have the whole business off your hands.

In fact if you do decide to do it all yourself, you will probably find it much less complicated than you first imagined. The basic rules are laid out here, as well as some of the more detailed information which you can refer to as you need. Don't worry if you don't understand it all. Indeed, don't even try. No one in the world finds 'National Insurance Contribution Compensation on Statutory Sick Pay' an easy concept! The best idea is to master the standard procedure for PAYE before your nanny starts and to leave the finer points of sick pay and the rest until you need them. After all, your nanny may never be ill long enough for you to operate the sick pay scheme. So it would be a complete waste of energy for you to spend a long time puzzling over it.

For detailed points you may contact your local Inland Revenue and Social Security Offices. They usually try to be helpful – after all they are keen to encourage people to pay their contributions properly! But they are often under-staffed and over-worked, so you may need some patience before you get your own particular queries sorted out. Another source of reference is the series of official 'Employer's guides', which deal at some length with the procedures for assessing and paying the various contributions.

PAYE – Income Tax and National Insurance

The basic principle of the PAYE (Pay As You Earn) system is very simple. You start from your nanny's full pay before any deductions (her *gross* pay) and you work out how much tax she owes on that and what her own (employee's) contribution to National Insurance will be. You then deduct those figures from her gross wage to give you her *net* pay. This smaller amount is what she actually *takes home*. Every quarter you add up the total of those deductions and you send it as a cheque to the Collector of Taxes (Accounts Office), together with your own (employer's) contribution to her National Insurance. Note that you just have to send off one cheque to the Collector of Taxes for all the contributions, even though National Insurance departments and the Inland Revenue (Income Tax) are in other respects separate. You simply record on the paying-in slip how much of the cheque is for tax and how much for National Insurance.

If you are paying your nanny a very low wage, she may not reach the thresholds at which she is liable for tax and National Insurance contributions. The details of these thresholds are available from your local Inland Revenue Office. But for the rest of this section it is assumed that you will be paying your nanny more than the lower qualifying limit. If you are not, you can skip the next few pages – but you should ask yourself whether she really has enough to live on!

Before she starts

As soon as you have found a nanny and agreed her gross pay and her starting date, get in touch with your local office (PAYE Section) of the Inland Revenue (Inspector of Taxes). You may phone to get things moving, but it is best to follow it up with a letter (and keep a copy for yourself). You should tell the office that you are about to take on an employee whose tax and insurance you want to pay on the 'Simplified System' (a scheme specially designed to make things easier for small domestic employers). They will need to know:

- the nanny's surname and first two christian names
- the title of her job (this will normally be 'nanny')
- her National Insurance number (if she does not know it, the Inland Revenue or Social Security Office will tell you how to find it out)
- the date she starts the job
- her gross pay (and whether it is to be paid weekly or monthly)
- the nanny's home address
- the name and address of her last employer.

In addition, if the nanny gives you a form P45 from her last employer ('Employee leaving – copy of Employer's Certificate'), you should send this straight away to the Inland Revenue Office. If the nanny cannot for any reason produce a P45 (if, for example, it is her first job), you should tell the local tax office. They will then send a form P46 for her to complete. But don't delay sending off the other information while you wait for either of these forms.

You will receive in return a large bundle of forms and information. The most important of these will be the 'Simplified Deduction Card' (P12), the instruction leaflet 'How to fill in the Simplified Deduction Card' (P16), the 'National Insurance Contribution Tables' (CF391) and a book of payslips for returning your cheque every quarter (P30BC(Q)(Z)) with some reply-paid envelopes. But you will probably also be sent some of the 'Employer's guides' (to Pay As You Earn (P7), to National Insurance Contributions (NP15) and to Statutory Sick Pay (NI227)), 'Statutory Sick Pay Rates and Notes' (SSP55), a form to record the details of your 'business', and maybe a blank form P45, which you will not need until your nanny *leaves* your employment. The Simplified Deduction Card will already have details of your nanny written in. It will also record her tax code and the amount of her 'free pay' – that is, the amount of her gross monthly or weekly wage on which she *does not* have to pay tax (see the example on pp. 78-9). This card will be the basis for *all* your calculations – for income tax, National Insurance and Statutory Sick Pay.

To find out how much tax to deduct

You will need just the Simplified Deduction Card and the instruction leaflet (P16). The instructions themselves are rather sketchy for an absolute beginner (not to say hopelessly inadequate). But the leaflet also includes the 'Simplified Tax Tables', which are an essential part of the whole process. The example on pp. 78-9 shows you exactly how to fill in the card.

Every week (or month) you enter in the column marked 'pay day' the exact date on which you give the nanny her wages. In column 2 you put the full amount of her *gross pay*, before any deductions. You write in column 3 the amount of 'free pay' (as recorded in the top left-hand corner of the card) – and then subtract the figure in column 3 (free pay) from the figure in column 2 (gross pay) and enter the result in column 4 ('taxable pay in the week or month'). This gives you the amount of your nanny's pay which is liable for tax. You then turn to the Simplified Tax Tables which will tell you how much tax she actually has to pay on that amount. They are very simple. You just look in the tables for the figure you have written in your column 4 (or if it is not there, then the next lowest figure) – and listed beside it you will find the amount that you must deduct for tax from her gross pay. You then write this in column 5.

When you give your nanny her wages, you will subtract this sum (as well as her National Insurance contribution) from her gross pay. You must by law provide her with a written statement of these deductions. This need only take the form of a hand-written note given to her with her pay, recording her gross wages and the amounts deducted for tax and National Insurance.

You may have some doubts about what actually counts as the nanny's gross pay. If you pay her extra for babysitting, does that count? What if you give her money for her fares to

How to fill in a Simplified Deduction Card

Copy of one quarter's entries on a Simplified Deduction Card

Employee's National Insurance No.	Employee's date of birth *in figures*			Enter here	Nature of employment	**1988-89**
AB 12 34 56 C	Day 00	Month 07	Year 07	'M' if male 'F' if female — F	NANNY	**Simplified Deduction Card**

Employee's Surname in CAPITAL letters	First two forenames	Employee's private address
BROWN	MARY LOUISE	7 REGENT'S DRIVE, LANCHESTER

Tax District and reference	Employer's name and address
BRIDGETOWN 2	JANE SMITH, CROFT LODGE, BRIDGETOWN

Code 200T

Free Pay £ 50·18 per *week/*month *Delete as necessary

	National Insurance Contributions						Pay Day	Total pay in the week or month including Statutory Sick Pay/ Statutory Maternity Pay 2	Free pay in the week or month 3	Taxable pay in the week or month 4	Tax deducted in the week or month 5
	Earnings on which employee's contributions payable 1a	Total of employee's and employer's contributions payable 1b	Employee's contributions payable 1c	Statutory Sick Pay in the week or month included in Column 2 1d	Statutory Maternity Pay in the week or month included in Column 2 1e						
†When you make the first entry on the card or when there is a change of table letter enter letter showing contribution table you have used.	90 00	12 00	6 55	£	£	£	5·4·88	90 00	50 18	39 82	9 75
	90 00	12 00	6 55				15·4	90 00	50 18	39 82	9 75
	90 00	12 00	6 55				22·4	90 00	50 18	39 82	9 75
	90 00	12 00	6 55				29·4	90 00	50 18	39 82	9 75
	90 00	12 00	6 55				6·5	90 00	50 18	39 82	9 75
	90 00	12 00	6 55				13·5	90 00	50 18	39 82	9 75
	90 00	12 00	6 55				20·5	90 00	50 18	39 82	9 75
	90 00	12 00	6 55				27·5	90 00	50 18	39 82	9 75
	90 00	12 00	6 55				3·6	90 00	50 18	39 82	9 75
	90 00	12 00	6 55				10·6	90 00	50 18	39 82	9 75
	90 00	12 00	6 55		49 20		17·6	90 00	50 18	39 82	9 75
	90 00	12 00	6 55				24·6	90 00	50 18	39 82	9 75
NI Totals Enter in columns 1a, 1b and 1c separate totals for each table used.	90 00	12 00	6 55				1·7	90 00	50 18	39 82	9 75
†N.I. Cont'n Table Letter — A	1170 00	164 00	52 20		49 20			1170 00			126 75

| TOTALS for quarter ending 5 JULY 1988 ▶ | 1170 00 | 164 00 | 52 20 | | 49 20 | | | 1170 00 | | | 126 75 |

You will find that all the details at the top of the card (including the amount of Free Pay) have already been completed when you receive the card. You normally have to fill in just the figures for pay and deductions each week, and add up the totals at the end of each quarter.

The example shown here is of a nanny, Mary Brown, paid £90.00 per week.

Tax. Mary's free pay amounts to £50.18 (col. 3), which leaves £39.82 on which she has to pay tax (col. 4). This means (col. 5) £9.75 tax to be paid from her wages each week.

National Insurance. A National Insurance contribution is payable on the full £90.00 of Mary's wages (col. 1a). This comes to £12.66 altogether per week (col. 1b), of which £6.33 can be deducted by Jane from her nanny's pay (col. 1c). (Jane herself must pay the other £6.33. But this figure is not entered separately on the card – simply included in the total of col. 1b.)

Statutory Sick Pay. For one whole week of the quarter Mary was ill. So she received £49.20 SSP (col. 1d). But note that her total pay for that week (col. 2) remained the same – £90.00. This is because, at the start of the employment, Jane agreed to make up Mary's state sick pay to her normal full wages, at least for the first two weeks of illness.

The end of the quarter. At the end of the quarter Jane Smith would normally send to the Collector of Taxes the total of tax deducted (col. 5 – £126.75) and the total joint National Insurance contributions (col. 1b – £164.58). But in this case she can hold back from the National Insurance contributions the amount of SSP she has paid (col. 1d – £49.20), as well as (if she remembers!) £3.44 – the 'National Insurance Contribution Compensation' on that amount (that is 7% of £49.20).

So she sends to the Collector of Taxes:

(a) Total tax = £126.75
(b) National Insurance contributions with deductions for SSP etc. = £111.94 (that is, £164.58 minus £52.64)
Grand total = £238.69

Remember: this is only an example to illustrate the general rules. Do not copy the figures even if you are paying your nanny £90.00 per week. Rates of tax and National Insurance contributions change regularly. And your nanny's Tax Code (which determines the amount of free pay) may be different from that chosen in this example.

and from work – do you have to include that in her pay that is liable for tax? Many people assume that these payments (often made in cash) are free of tax. In fact, this is not technically the case. And, if you act strictly according to the rules, all money given to your nanny for babysitting or for fares should be included on her card under 'total pay' in column 2. The only payments which a nanny might normally receive that are *not* liable to tax are payments for expenses she incurs *in the course of* her work. If, for example, she takes your child to the zoo and you reimburse her for the fare and entry fee, you do not need to include that in the figure in column 2.

To find out how much National Insurance to deduct

This is just as easy. You first of all enter her earnings 'on which employee's contributions are payable' in column 1a. This will be the same figure as you have written in column 2. There are, in theory, various kinds of payments (such as company cars and other perks) that might be liable for tax but not National Insurance. But these are not the kind of payments normally given to nannies – so you can pretty safely assume that the amount you write in column 1a will be exactly the same as that in column 2.

You then turn to your book of National Insurance Contribution Tables (CF391) to find out exactly how much money is owed. Your book will be labelled 'Non-contracted out contributions' – unless you have a private occupational pension scheme for your nanny! The only problem here is that the instructions in the front of the book will not always apply to you, as they are not written with the simplified system in mind. Make sure that you follow what is laid down in your instruction leaflet P16. In almost every case (unless you are employing someone over retirement age or a married woman who opted to pay a reduced National Insurance contribution *before 1977*) you will use just the first table in the book, Table A.

You find your nanny's gross pay in the left-hand column of the table (or the next lowest figure, if the exact amount is not there) and read across to find (a) the total National Insurance contribution payable (employee's and employer's contribution together) and (b) the amount of the contribution payable by the employee alone. You enter these figures in columns 1b and 1c of the Simplified Deduction Card. You *may* then deduct the employee's contribution (the amount in column 1c) from your nanny's gross wages – remembering to give her a written note of the amount, when you pay her (see p. 77). But, unlike the tax assessment, you do not *have* to make this deduction. You can pay it yourself, if you wish.

How to pay what you owe

At the end of each quarter (the dates are given on the Simplified Deduction Card), you just add up the figures in columns 1b and 5. This gives you the total amount of National Insurance and Income Tax owed for the last three months. And you send it off to the Collector of Taxes, Accounts Office, using the paying-in slips and reply-paid envelopes that are usually supplied. The paying-in slip will ask you to record how much of the cheque is for tax and how much for National Insurance.

This bill can easily amount to more than £200 a quarter. In theory you will have 'deducted' a lot of this from your nanny's pay. But, unless you really have put a bit of money on one side each week, the bill can come as quite a shock (especially if it coincides with the gas and electricity).

At the end of the tax year

The tax year ends on 5 April each year. At this point you send off your final quarter's cheque to the Collector of Taxes *and* you send the completed Deduction Card back to your local Tax Inspector (at the Inland Revenue Office). You will then be sent a Form P60 ('Certificate of Pay and Tax Deducted') to give to your nanny. This records the total amount of her pay, tax and employee's National Insurance contributions for the year.

If she leaves

If your nanny leaves, you add up the totals in columns 1b and 5 up to the date of her leaving and send a cheque off to the Collector of Taxes in the normal way. You send the Simplified Deduction Card back to your local tax office, filling in the date that the nanny left and the name and address of her new employer (if you know it). You should also give *to the nanny* a form P45 ('Employee leaving'), which records her pay and tax up to the date of her leaving. She needs this to give to her next employer.

If you make a mistake

The system is not as complicated as it sounds. Most people get the hang of it very quickly and very few make any serious mistake. But if you have been doing something wrong, it may not be spotted until the end of the tax year. The Inland Revenue will certainly get in touch with you. But the total error could be very large by then. If you have *over*-paid your nanny's contributions, the situation is not too serious. You will receive a refund. You may also like to compensate her in some way for the inconvenience of having had a lower take-home pay than she should have had! If, on the other hand, you have *under*-paid the tax, it is rather more difficult. There will be a bill for back-tax for which *you* are liable, not your nanny. The best thing to do is to go round to the local tax office, if you have time during their office hours. Take all the records of your nanny's employment and try and sort it out face to face. This is probably quicker in the long run than trying to handle the problem by phone or letter. It is also a good idea to try a personal visit, if you *ever suspect* your calculations may be going wrong. The earlier you discover any mistake, the less chance there is of building up a big bill for back-tax.

Saving on National Insurance

There is one place where you can save money on National Insurance contributions. Occasionally by paying your nanny a *smaller* gross wage, you can end up giving her a *bigger* take-home pay packet and paying less to the government. In order to work this out, you need to understand a little bit of the principles of National Insurance contributions.

Most people calculate their National Insurance contributions by referring to the easy published tables. But the payments are, in fact, based on a percentage of the employee's gross pay. And this percentage is 'banded' – so that a higher percentage is paid on the higher 'bands' of salary. These bands are laid out in the front of the Contribution Tables (CF391). For saving money, the essential point you need to know is this: once a salary has crossed into a higher band, the higher rate is payable on the *whole* amount, not just on the extra amount that goes into that band.

Suppose for example that the dividing line between 5 per cent and 7 per cent contributions comes at £69.99. If you were to pay your nanny £69, she would lose £3.47 in National Insurance (5 per cent). If you were to pay her £70, she would lose £4.93 (7 per cent). In other words a £1 increase in salary would be wiped out by £1.46 extra National Insurance. And you also would be paying the employer's contribution at that higher rate. Everyone (apart from the taxman) will be better off if you pay her the lower amount.

The message is – do your sums very carefully when you are fixing a salary close to the edge of one of the percentage bands.

STATUTORY SICK PAY (SSP)

If your nanny is ill, you may have to pay her Statutory Sick Pay. This is government sick pay which *you pay* as employer – and then *reimburse yourself* by holding back some of the National Insurance contributions that you would normally have paid. The principle is quite simple. If you have to pay £20 to your nanny in Statutory Sick Pay, you will send £20 less than usual to the Collector of Taxes at the end of the quarter. The details of the scheme can be complicated. They are laid out at length in the relevant 'Employer's guide' – although this is not written with the simplified scheme in mind, so is occasionally misleading. But the general rules can easily be explained.

If your nanny is ill and off work for three days or less you should continue to pay her normal wages. But if she is sick for four consecutive days or more (up to a period of twenty-eight weeks) she will normally qualify for Statutory Sick Pay. This is not full pay, but a flat rate sum paid at one of three levels (according to the employee's gross pay). These rates are revised in April each year and are published in 'SSP Rates and Notes' (SSP55), which can be obtained from any Social Security Office if it was not sent to you with your Simplified Deduction Card.

You should have no problem deciding whether your nanny really is sick. If she is living with you, it will be obvious anyway. If she lives out, it is a bit more difficult. But, unless relations between you have really broken down, a quick phone call from her to say 'I'm ill' is probably going to be enough – at least for the first few days. Remember you have no right to ask her for a doctor's note until she has been away for more than seven days.

How much sick pay your nanny actually receives will depend on you and on whatever agreement you have with her. You *can* just pay her the appropriate rate of Statutory Sick Pay (out of your own pocket in the first instance). That is quite legal. But you may decide to make up that amount to her normal full wage, at least for one or two weeks. This must be agreed with her in principle when she starts the job – and, in fact, it is a legal requirement that you tell her in writing how much sick pay she will receive and over what period (see p. 94). Most people think it reasonable to make up her wage beyond the level of SSP for a few weeks at the beginning of each period of illness. But remember – you will not be reimbursed for any amount you give her above SSP and you may need to take on additional temporary paid help (or take unpaid leave yourself) while she is sick. Be fair to your nanny, but don't bankrupt yourself!

Paying SSP makes a difference to how you fill in your Simplified Deduction Card and what you pay to the Collector of Taxes at the end of the quarter. On her pay day you enter

into column 2 in the normal way the total amount you have
paid her during the week (or month), *including any Statutory
Sick Pay* – but you *also* note in column 1d the amount of
Statutory Sick Pay alone that you have paid. These two figures
(in columns 2 and 1d) are likely to be different. In fact, they will
only be exactly the same if she has been receiving SSP for the
whole week and you have not been paying her any extra on
top of that. You fill in the rest of the card as usual, calculating
the tax and National Insurance contributions on her total pay
including SSP. If you do not make her wages up to their normal
level, she will of course pay less tax and National Insurance
than usual.

National Insurance contribution compensation on SSP

This is the only place where the system of deductions gets
really complicated – so complicated in fact that the latest
edition of the Contribution Tables complains that some
employers just aren't bothering with it! At the end of the
quarter, you add up the figures in column 1d, to find out the
total amount of SSP you have paid. You can then deduct that
amount from the National Insurance money you send to the
Collector of Taxes. You can also deduct a sum to compensate
for the employer's National Insurance contribution payable
on SSP – the so-called 'NIC compensation on SSP'. This may
seem an unnecessarily intricate detail. But SSP *is* counted
into the total pay on which National Insurance contributions
are levied. And if you were not allowed to make this
deduction, you would be in the ridiculous position of paying
to the government the 'employer's' contribution not on
wages paid *by you*, but on a government social security
benefit!

In order to calculate this deduction, you turn to the weeks
on your Deduction Card in which Statutory Sick Pay was paid
and add up the total amount of SSP paid during the quarter.
Find out (from the front of the Contribution Tables (CF391))
what percentage rate the compensation is made (it is
standardised across all rates of National Insurance contributions) – and deduct that percentage from the National

Insurance money you send to the Collector of Taxes.

Example

Suppose you have paid £135.53 SSP during the last quarter. And suppose that the percentage rate for compensation during the period was 7 per cent. You will deduct from your National Insurance payment to the Collector of Taxes:

- £135.53: the full amount of SSP
- £135.53 × 7 per cent = £9.49 (rounded to the nearest penny): NIC compensation on SSP

So you will deduct altogether £145.02!

Too much SSP?

Occasionally the amount you should deduct for SSP from your National Insurance contribution is greater than the contribution itself. If this is the case, you should deduct the excess from the tax contribution you pay that quarter. If the amount you should deduct turns out to be greater than the National Insurance and tax contributions put together, you pay nothing to the Collector of Taxes for that quarter – and you either deduct the rest next quarter, or you can ask the Collector of Taxes (address as on the payslip booklet) to reimburse you straight away.

Getting help with SSP

If you are lucky you will never have to operate the Statutory Sick Pay scheme. It does certainly seem more complicated than the standard tax and National Insurance system. This is partly because you do not (you hope!) do it regularly enough for it to become familiar. But it is also because *everything* seems more trouble when your childcare arrangements have broken down and you are trying desperately to find some way of continuing to work *and* get the children minded. Working out SSP would no doubt seem quite easy, if it did not necessarily come at a time when you are without your nanny! The best advice is to consult your local Social Security Office as soon as you begin to feel out of your depth and to keep a full record of exactly what you did and how you arrived at your figures (what you multiplied by what!). That way, the experts will be able to sort out your mistakes much more quickly. But take heart – most people do manage to operate the system completely successfully.

STATUTORY MATERNITY PAY

Don't forget that the boot may be on the other foot! If you have employed your nanny full-time for at least two years she will be normally be eligible for six weeks' maternity leave at 90 per cent of her full pay and twelve weeks at the lower rate of SMP. If she has been with you just six months or more, she will probably qualify for the lower rate of SMP for eighteen weeks. SMP is payable whether or not your nanny intends to return to work with you.

You will already be familiar with some of the intricacies of the system from your own case (see Chapter 1). As an employer, you will find that the scheme operates in much the same way as Statutory Sick Pay. That is to say, you pay your nanny SMP out of your own pocket in the first instance. You later reimburse yourself (for the full amount of the benefit, as well as the employer's National Insurance contributions on that amount) by deducting it from the cheque you send to the Collector of Taxes at the end of the quarter. Again, as with sick pay, it is up to you whether or not you make up your nanny's SMP to the level of her normal wage, and for how long. You will no doubt be torn in two ways. On the one hand, you will almost certainly need to take on a new nanny (either permanently or temporarily), and on top of *her* salary you may not be able to afford to give much extra to your old employee. On the other hand, you will be shamed by the inconsistency of demanding better maternity rights for yourself from your *employers*, while paying your *employee* just the mean legal allowance! Be as generous as you can.

But work out in advance how generous you can afford to be *realistically*.

TAX IN A NANNY-SHARE

If you are going to be sharing a nanny with another family, consult your local tax office in advance. The arrangement you make will depend on the particular circumstances of your 'share' and on the normal practice of your tax office – which can differ from one office to another. You are likely to have one of three different arrangements. They each have slightly different implications for the tax and National Insurance you, and your nanny, will be paying.

- You and your sharing partner may be regarded as *joint employers* of your nanny. In this case, you will pay tax and National Insurance in the ordinary way. And it will be up to you to decide how to divide the expenses between you.
- You and your partner could enter *separate contracts* with the nanny (for, say, half the total salary each). In this case the total amount paid in tax would remain the same, but there would be a difference in the National Insurance. That would be assessed on each separate contract – so almost certainly would remain in a lower percentage band than the combined salary.

    For example, if each partner was paying £60 per week, then National Insurance would be levied (on the 1988 scale) at the rate of 5 per cent for each contract – a deduction of £6.04 from her total weekly salary and £3.02 from each employer. If the nanny was receiving a single salary of £120, she (and her employers) would be paying contributions at 9 per cent – that is £10.84 per week from both nanny and employers.

    It could even be that each half contract did not reach the level at which National Insurance was payable at all. This would, of course, be a substantial saving. But, in this case, the nanny should be advised to pay the small *voluntary* contributions needed to protect her rights to a state retirement pension.

- In some nanny shares, it might be appropriate to count the nanny as self-employed. You and your partner then become technically her clients. In this case, she takes care of her own tax and you do not have to pay employer's contribution towards National Insurance – because you are not actually her employer. This relieves you of all the paper-work (which is handled by the nanny herself), and on the surface you have less to pay. But you may find that your nanny asks for more money – which would cancel out any big saving.

You almost certainly cannot decide yourself how to pay the right contributions in a nanny-share. You must get in touch with your tax office, explain to them your own circumstances and let them advise. Alternatively, consult an accountant. He or she may be able to work out a favourable scheme for you – and convince the Inland Revenue that it is appropriate.

EMPLOYER'S OBLIGATIONS

There is an enormous amount of complicated legislation regulating the terms of any employment and protecting the rights of employees. There is absolutely no need for you to become an expert in all this before you start to employ a nanny. But it is a good idea to grasp a few basic points. You ought to realise from the very beginning that you cannot simply hire and fire at whim!

Many of the laws can look a bit frightening from the point of view of a new employer. They talk about penalties, industrial tribunals, claims for 'unfair dismissal' and the rest. For most people, most of the time, these things will never become an issue. And many of the legal provisions and penalties are simply inappropriate to small 'domestic' employers. But it is a good idea to follow the rules as closely as you can – and not just for the sake of being law-abiding.

There are two particular reasons for this. The first is self-interested realism. *Very, very occasionally* relations between employer and nanny break down completely – the nanny leaves amid seething emotions and bad feeling. In this situation, when all kinds of threats are bandied around from one party to the other, it is important to know that you have fulfilled the employer's side of the bargain correctly. It is extremely unlikely that she would even threaten to take you to law. But there is no point in putting yourself in a position in which you worry about that, because you have not actually obeyed the employment rules.

The second reason is more for the sake of guidance. You most likely have never employed anyone before and have no very precise idea what fair practice on the part of an employer amounts to. It is in fact very difficult to change your attitude from that of an *employee* (as you are most of the time) to that of an *employer* (as you are in relation to your nanny). The great advantage of the legal rules is that they give you an idea of the *minimum acceptable* terms of employment. If you follow them (and particularly if you are a bit more generous) you can be fairly confident that you are acting as a 'reasonable' employer.

Written statement of main terms and conditions of employment

The main obligation that you have at the start of your nanny's employment is to provide her with a written statement of her main terms and conditions of employment. The law here is quite clear – even if a bit bizarre to the outsider! The law regards *every employee* as having a *contract* with his or her employer. But this does not have to be written down to be legally binding. As soon as an employee accepts a job he or she is deemed to have entered into a contract with the employer – on the terms that were verbally agreed and on other 'implied' terms (based on requirements laid down by law and normal practice in the profession concerned). What *must be written down* (within thirteen weeks of the job starting) is a *statement* of the main terms and conditions of the employment. This is not technically a 'contract', although, in practice, it usually represents the bare bones of the contract (whether written or not).

These legal technicalities can cause some confusion. You

will sometimes hear a nanny complain that she 'does not have a contract' with her employers. She is wrong. By definition, she had a contract (even if unwritten) from the moment she accepted the job. What she normally means is that her boss has failed to provide her with any written particulars of her job. She has in fact a legal right to demand these.

The contents of the written statement

The law is quite specific about what the written statement must contain. It falls into three parts:

- The first records the name of the employer and employee, the date on which the job started and whether any previous employment counts as 'continuous employment' with this job (and, if so, the date on which that employment started).
- The second should record the title of the job concerned, the rate of pay (and whether it is paid weekly or monthly), the hours of work, holiday entitlement, sickness arrangements and pay, and details of any pension scheme and the length of notice to be given by employee and employer.
- The third adds a statement on any disciplinary rules in force and how the employee should raise any grievances. It should also state whether or not a 'contracting-out' certificate is in force for the employment concerned (allowing lower National Insurance contributions in the case of certain occupational pension schemes).

Most of this information is entirely straightforward. But some clauses require rather more difficult decisions than it might appear at first sight. You would have to sort out most of these issues at some point anyway (matters of holiday pay, for example, or making up SSP to the full wage). Providing the written particulars gives you a good incentive to do it straight away. After all, you do not want to find yourself with a nanny who has booked a *three*-week holiday – when you had always imagined (though never actually *said*) that she would take just *two*.

Continuous employment

The issue of 'continuous employment' is important in law –
because the longer someone has worked with the same
employer, the more rights they have. For example, the right
to reinstatement after maternity leave depends on two years'
continuous service with the same employer. It is *extremely
unlikely* that your nanny's previous job will count as
'continuous employment' with the job you are offering her.
The only plausible exception comes in the case of nanny
shares. Suppose, for example, you start out sharing a nanny
with a friend – but she drops out of the arrangement while
you continue to employ the nanny (either on your own or in a
new partnership). The nanny's continuous employment
would probably be counted back to the start of the first nanny
share and you should say so in the written particulars. ('Your
employment with me began on (date). Your previous
employment with myself and (name) counts as part of your
continuous period of employment, which therefore began on
(date).')

Job title

Bear in mind the differences between 'nanny' and 'mother's
help'. If you are having no other job description, remember
that someone called 'nanny' will not normally expect to do
general household work. For someone called 'mother's help',
that will be a standard part of the job.

Hours of work

Think carefully about how long you want the nanny to work
and whether you want it to be the same each week. A mother
with a 9 to 5 job near her home might be happy with a regular
working week for her nanny of 8.30 to 5.30. But do not cut
the hours so fine that you end up never quite getting back on
time – or so that you never have a 'handover' period at the
beginning or end of the day (see p. 144). You do not want to
exploit your nanny with ridiculously long hours. But equally

you will be doing her no favour by stating hours that you can never, realistically, keep to. Some mothers will want a degree of flexibility. If you are a teacher, for example, you may want the nanny to work longer hours during term than during the vacation. If you are working changing shifts, you will obviously want her hours to change with yours. One useful way of ensuring flexibility is to specify just a certain maximum number of hours a week and broad guide-lines on the time (say 'forty-two hours a week between the hours of 7.30 am and 8.30 pm'). You can then arrange her exact hours week by week. But make sure you do it in advance – otherwise she will never be able to plan any social life.

If you have a live-in nanny, you should state clearly in the written particulars how many week-ends you will want her to work and how many evenings babysitting you will require each week. Do not automatically assume that you will normally want week-end work from your nanny. Some live-ins like to go away then. And even if it means more work for you, there are advantages. *You* get a chance to be a family. *She* comes back having had a break from you and the kids (see also pp. 108-10).

You should also make clear in your written statement how you will treat overtime. If you want to be able to *insist* that your nanny works longer hours when you need it, this should be explicitly stated. Make sure you also state the maximum number of extra hours you will require from her and the rate of pay. The other option is simply to state that overtime will be arranged by mutual agreement.

Holiday entitlement

Every employee will assume that they can be off work on the public holidays (Christmas Day, Boxing Day, etc). If you will ever require your nanny to work on one of these days, you must state that in the written particulars. And it would be normal in that case to offer a day off in lieu of the holiday worked. Your nanny will expect a reasonable amount of paid holiday in addition to the public holidays – at least fourteen days and often longer. But think carefully before you just

write down 'twenty-one days holiday a year'. Will she have
free choice of when she takes her time off? Do you want to
specify, for example, that she chooses time during the school
holidays? Or do you even want to be able to designate
precise days that she must take as holiday (suppose you go
away on *your* holidays without her...). When does your
'holiday year' start? And will she be able to carry days over
from one year to the next? Will she be offered further days of
unpaid holiday?

Sickness arrangements

You should state that you will operate the Statutory Sick Pay
scheme (see pp. 83-7). If you intend to be more generous
than this, lay out the terms exactly. You may, for example,
decide that you will make up SSP to her full wage for two
weeks in her first year of employment and for three weeks
from the second year. Or you might decide to offer 75 per
cent of full pay for a month. There are any number of
possibilities. Decide on one and stick to it.

You should also make clear what kind of evidence you will
accept as proof of sickness. Say at what point you may
require that she produce a doctor's certificate (though
remember (p. 84) that you cannot by law demand such a
certificate before she has been ill for seven days).

Pension scheme

Very, very few employers of private nannies will offer an
occupational pension scheme. But you should state clearly
that no pension scheme is in force.

Notice

Employers normally ask that their nannies give them a
month's notice that they intend to leave. This is a good
general principle – and you would almost certainly need all
that time to find a permanent replacement (see pp. 113-15).
But remember that there is *in practice* nothing you can do

actually to keep your nanny at work if she wants to leave suddenly. There is certainly not much point in asking for any longer period of notice. It might *look* as if you would get more time to find somebody new. But nine times out of ten it would be difficult (and maybe unreasonable) to make your old nanny work out her full notice – so nothing is gained. For the legal minimum periods of notice, see pp. 102-3. It is a good idea to have a probationary period (no longer than a month) during which either side can withdraw more quickly.

Disciplinary rules and grievances

If you employ just one person in your home, you will obviously not have any complex procedure for discipline at work or for your nanny to raise grievances. Nevertheless the law requires that you state what you intend to do if problems arise. In the case of discipline, it is the normal practice to say that you will first give an oral warning, then a written warning, then dismissal. But both sides will have to be realistic over this. Nannying depends on complete trust. If you get so far as a formal oral warning, you can be fairly certain that your nanny will not want to stay with you much longer. A grievance procedure is also out of place in this kind of job. Just say that all grievances should be referred directly to the employers!

Contracting-out certificate

It is almost certain that you will not run an occupational pension scheme which will allow your nanny to pay lower National Insurance contributions (so-called 'contracting-out'). Simply state 'A contracting-out certificate under the Social Security Pensions Act 1975 is not in force for this employment'.

The bare essentials: an example

You can if you like buy pre-printed forms, which lay out all this information – leaving you to fill in the particular details of your job. But if you want to write yourself, to give your nanny the legal minimum of written particulars, it is very simple. Your letter might look something like the example below. The details will, of course, differ according to the type of job. The example given is written for a live-out job. The particulars for a live-in nanny would no doubt lay down rather more complicated arrangements on hours of work. But the overall format would be the same.

Croft Lodge
Bridgetown
18 December 1988

Dear Mary,

This letter sets out the main terms and conditions on which I (Jane Smith) am employing you (Mary Brown). Your employment with me will begin on 1 January 1989. No previous employment will count as part of your period of continuous employment.

1. You are employed as nanny.

2. Your pay will be £90 per week (payable weekly in arrears). Overtime will be paid at £2.50 per hour.

3. Your normal hours of week will be 8.30 am to 6.00 pm, Monday to Friday. Overtime will be by mutual agreement.

4. You will have all public holidays as holiday (apart from the May Day holiday – for which you may take another day off in lieu, by arrangement). In addition you are entitled to 21 days paid holiday (to be taken during periods of school holidays). The holiday year runs from 1 January to 31 December and holidays cannot be carried over from one year to the next.

5. I shall operate the Statutory Sick Pay scheme. In addition I shall make up that pay to the amount of your normal wage for the first two weeks of any period of sickness. I may ask you to provide me with a doctor's certificate if your illness lasts more than seven days.

6. No pension scheme will operate in this employment.

7. During the first month of your employment one week's notice will be required on either side. From the second month on, the period of notice will be one month.

In the event of any need for discipline, the procedure will be: first – oral warning; second – written warning; and third – dismissal. If you have any grievance you should bring it directly to me.

A contracting out certificate under the Social Security Pensions Act 1975 is not in force for this employment.

Yours sincerely,
Jane Smith.

Remember that these details, in their skeletal form, look rather stern and off-putting. If you are sending them to a nanny you have just appointed, you should enclose a friendly covering letter – explaining that you are giving her these details because it is required by law *and* because it is a good idea to get things like this put in writing. Apologise for looking so formal. And tell her to get in touch with you if there is anything she wants to query. It is important to provide these written particulars as is required by law. But you do not want to *terrify* an eighteen-year-old straight from college by stark references to disciplinary procedures and grievances!

A fuller contract

Some people prefer to incorporate the written particulars into a fuller 'contract' which gives more detail on the duties of the job and household arrangements. They make two copies – one for themselves and one for the nanny. Each is signed by both sides and then kept as a record of what was agreed at the start of the job.

This is a good idea – because it makes both sides think carefully about what the job will mean and then put their signatures to it. It also gives you an easy way of raising some possible areas of disagreement at the very start. Are you going to let the nanny use the phone freely – or just for local calls? If she is living in will she be welcome to eat with you always? Or on just some occasions? You should put down in writing the points that seem most important to you. These will obviously vary from family to family. Simply follow your own instincts. If, for example, you are an Orthodox Jewish family and insist on dietary rules – do make this absolutely clear in the contract. Or if your child has a complicated course of medication that she must always follow, you should spell this out.

But do not *overestimate* what a contract of this kind will do for you. You will normally include only broad guidelines about the care of your child. Unless there was some very pressing reason, it would be absolutely crazy to state that she should always serve lunch to the child at 12.30 or that she

Contract for a live-in nanny: an example

Contract of employment as nanny
between
Jane Smith (the employer)   and
Croft Lodge,   Mary Brown (the employee)
Bridgetown   7 Regent's Drive, Lanchester

with effect from 1.1.89
on which date the employment is to begin.
(No previous employment counts as part of the continuous period of employment.)

Duties: The employee is employed as nanny to the children of the employer – Zoe Smith (born 26.10.85) and Raphael Smith (born 24.7.87). She is required to undertake all necessary duties with regard to the health, welfare, education and daily care of the children during working hours. This may include outings for play and social activities, as seem desirable, and shopping for items necessary for the children. She is responsible for washing her own and the children's feeding utensils and for clearing up after the children's play. She will also wash, iron and repair (if necessary) the children's clothes. She is expected to keep the children busy and amused in accordance with the wishes of the parents.

The employment is based in Bridgetown. But the employee will be expected to accompany the employers on travel abroad and within the UK, for which all expenses will be paid.

Hours of work: The normal working week is from 8.30 am to 6.00 pm Monday to Friday. In addition the employee will be expected to babysit on up to two evenings a week (between Monday night and Friday night) from 7.00 pm onwards. These evenings will normally be notified at least one week in advance. Overtime will be by mutual agreement.

The hours of the working week may be altered when the employee is accompanying her employers on travel.

Holidays: The employee will be entitled to twenty-one days paid holiday a year (in addition to the public holidays). Seven of these days may be designated by the employer. Holidays may not be carried over into a new year. The holiday year runs from 1 January to 31 December.

Pay: The pay will be £90 per week, payable weekly in arrears. Tax and Employee's National Insurance contribution will be deducted from this sum. The pay will be reviewed on 5 April 1989 and annually thereafter.

Sick pay: In the case of incapacity to work due to sickness or injury, the employee shall be allowed 3 days' consecutive absence without loss of pay. Thereafter the employer will operate the Statutory Sick Pay scheme. In addition, during the first year of employment the employer will make up the sickness pay to the normal rate of pay for a maximum of four weeks; after one year of employment this period will be extended to eight weeks. The employee will be asked to produce a doctor's certificate after seven days' absence.

Pension scheme: No pension scheme is provided by the employer.

Household arrangements: The employee is entitled to live at Croft Lodge, Bridgetown at all times during her working week and (if she wishes) during her free time. Food, heating, electricity and bed linen will be provided for her free of charge. In addition she may have use of the appliances of the house (washing machine, iron etc). Her own room is for her own use as she pleases; although she should not make a noise so as to disturb other members of the household after 11 pm, and she should obtain prior permission for substantial gatherings of friends and overnight guests. She will have free use of the common parts of the house (kitchen, bathroom, etc) and will often be welcome to use the main sitting room; however, this may sometimes be needed for the employer's sole use. She will normally be welcome to eat as part of the familiy if she wishes. She may make free use of the telephone for calls connected with her work and for local personal calls. She will be expected to keep a record of any long-distance personal calls and to pay for them at the time of the quarterly bill.

Probationary period and notice: There will be an initial probationary period of four weeks from the date of commencement of the contract. During this period one week's notice is required on either side. Otherwise the amount of notice to be given by employer or employee is four weeks.

Discipline and grievances: In the event of the need to take disciplinary action against the employee the procedure will be: first – oral warning; second – written warning; third – dismissal.

Any grievances should be brought directly to the employer.

Contracting-out: A contracting-out certificate under the Social Security Pensions Act 1975 is not in force for this employment.

Signed: Jane Smith 11 December 1988
      Mary Brown 13 December 1988

Contract for a live-out nanny: an example

Contract of employment as nanny

Employer: Jane Smith, Croft Lodge, Bridgetown.

Employee: Mary Brown, 7, Regent's Drive, Lanchester.

Contract issued: 11 December, 1988.

Date employment is to start: 1 January, 1989. No previous employment counts as part of the period of continuous employment.

Title of job: Nanny.

Duties The employee is employed to take day-time charge of Zoe Smith and a baby expected in July 1989.

Salary: The salary is £5,200 per annum (payable weekly in arrears). Tax and Employee's National Insurance contribution will be deducted from this sum. The pay will be reviewed at the birth of the second child and yearly thereafter.

Hours of work: The hours of work are 8.15 am to 5.45 pm, Monday to Friday. In addition the employer may require up to three hours overtime per week (between 5.45 and 7.00 pm). Overtime beyond that will be by mutual agreement.

Holidays: The employee may take all public holidays as holiday. In addition she will be entitled to 21 days paid holiday per year (from January 1). Holidays may only be carried over to the next year by agreement with the employer. No compensaton will be given for holidays not taken. In the final year of service, paid holiday will be taken on a pro rata basis.

Sickness: The employer will operate the government Statutory Sick Pay Scheme. In addition she will make sickness benefit up to the normal wage for the first four weeks of any period of sickness.

Pension: No pension scheme is operated by the employer.

Probationary period: The employee is employed for a probationary period of four weeks.

Termination: In the first four weeks of employment, one week's notice is required. Thereafter the contract may be terminated by employer or employee with four weeks notice.

Conduct and discipline: The following actions may give rise to disciplinary action:

(a)   Failure to comply with the employer's instructions for care of the child/children.

(b)   Unpunctuality.

(c)   Breaching the confidentiality of the household.

(d)   Failure to exercise due care with the possessions and household effects of the employer.

In the case of disciplinary action, the procedure is: first – oral warning; second – written warning; third – dismissal.

Summary dismissal may follow any action which endangers the safety of the child/children.

Grievances: Any grievance is to be referred directly to the employer.

Contracting-out: A contracting-out certificate under the Social Security Pensions Act 1975 is not in force for this employment.

Signed: Jane Smith   Mary Brown

should never allow her to have sweets. Over the time that she is with you, the child's routines and needs will change – and so will your attitudes to what is best. Besides, you are employing a nanny whom you will trust to look after your child in a caring and responsible way – not to follow a rule book.

Do not also be over-optimistic about the kind of legal protection that a contract will give you. You are not going to take legal action against your nanny because you found her telephoning her friends in New York, when you had specified that it was local calls only! You will not even be sacking her for that – unless it is the absolute last straw in a whole series of problems!

The real advantage of a contract is that it provides an agreed framework within which you both can work. The two examples set out on pp. 98-100 (one for a live-in, one for a live-out nanny) are quite different in type. They are not meant as models for what you should say. But both give some idea of what areas *might* be covered by such a document and how it might be laid out. Many of the topics included are to do with practical day-to-day living – and they are discussed in greater detail in the next chapter. But remember also that (unless you decide to issue *separate* 'written particulars') you must put in all the information that the law says should be included in the formal written statement of the main terms and conditions of employment (above, pp. 90-7).

These contracts are somewhat less stark than the formal written particulars of terms and conditions of employment. But they can still seem a bit aggressive and forbidding. You may feel awkward or even silly writing clauses about 'punctuality' and 'summary dismissal' – or referring to yourself as 'the employer' and your new nanny as 'the employee'. After all you are wanting to treat her as a *friend*, not a *servant*. That is all very well. And in the best of all worlds your nanny *will* become your friend. But you do no one any good by trying to *deny* that you are her employer. You *can* sack her. You *do* want her to be punctual. You *will* get cross if she persistently puts your child in the car without a child restraint. It is much the best to get some of this in writing

before you start. A good professional nanny will prefer it that
way. And it will not stop her becoming your friend!

THE END OF EMPLOYMENT

It is almost bound to be a sad time when your nanny leaves.
She may well be leaving with no ill feeling, at the end of a
long and happy time with you. But she will almost inevitably
miss you and (even more) the kids – and they will be sad to
see her go. Occasionally nannies leave in far less easy
circumstances – resigning suddenly, fed up or even sacked.
At these times (even more than on other occasions) the basic
legal rules about length of notice, reasons for dismissal and so
forth will provide some kind of framework to keep everything
as orderly as possible. The law cannot work miracles. It
cannot turn a sad occasion into a happy one. But it will give
you guidelines to follow and will, with luck, help you avoid
unnecessary bitterness.

Notice

The law lays down the *minimum* period of notice you must
give to your employee. You can, of course, give her more
notice than this. But if your contract specifies a shorter period
than the legal minimum, it is automatically overridden by the
regulations. The period varies according to the length of time
she has worked for you:

- If you have employed a nanny for more than a month, but
  less than two years, she is entitled to at least one week's
  notice.
- If you have employed her for two years, she is entitled to
  two weeks' notice.
- If you have employed her for more than two years, she is
  entitled to one extra week's notice for every year of her
  employment (up to a maximum of twelve).

You do not actually have to provide her with work during
these periods of notice. But if you do not, you must give her
her normal wages in lieu of notice.

The legal obligations on the nanny to provide *you* with notice are much less stringent. Once she has been employed by you for one month, she is required to provide one week's notice. Though again, a longer period may be laid down in your contract.

If any of these regulations are broken, there is not much in practice to be done. Your nanny could try to bring a civil action against you for breach of contract. But that would hardly be worth the effort. And for you, the only practical reply to a girl who left without warning would be to refuse to give her a reference. The point about sticking to the legal rules is that they act as a basic employment guide – not because dreadful penalties await if you do not.

Summary dismissal

This does not mean that if you come home to find your nanny completely deranged and attacking your screaming infant you cannot dismiss her straight away. Instant (or 'summary') dismissal is allowed where the employee has behaved so badly that it strikes 'at the root of the employment contract'. In the case of a private nanny any action that deliberately harmed the child or breached her position of trust within the family (walking off with the family jewels!) would easily justify instant dismissal.

Written reasons for dismissal

If your nanny has worked with you for at least six months, she has a right to ask you for written reasons why she is being dismissed. But you do not have to provide these *unless* she requests them.

Unfair dismissal and redundancy payments

Once your nanny has worked for you for two years she is protected by legislation that outlaws unfair dismissal and by provisions for redundancy pay.

It is exceedingly unlikely that any nanny would think it

worth her while to take a case for unfair dismissal before an industrial tribunal. This is partly because it is exceedingly unlikely that she would win. A small domestic employer can almost always show that dismissal was 'fair' – especially in a job such as nannying, where you can quite reasonably claim that the right temperament and personality are important elements in the job. But remember, if she does bring a case (whether she wins or not), you will have all the details of your employment exposed in public. If you were paying her little extras in cash, the taxman will be bound to find out.

'Redundancy' calls to mind big industry and mass lay-offs. But there is one circumstance when a nanny might be dismissed because she is technically 'redundant' – because there is no job left for her to do. That is, when your children start full-time school or nursery. Obviously you will have foreseen this a long way ahead and you will have discussed it with the nanny. There should be no question of her being taken by surprise or of going to law to obtain redundancy payments. But the levels of payment established by law in the case of redundancy provide some guide to how you might decide to compensate your nanny, They are:

- half a week's pay for every year worked between the ages of eighteen and twenty-one; and between the ages of forty-one and sixty (sixty-five for men).
- a week's pay for every year worked between twenty-two and forty-one.

You might even convince the DHSS that you are entitled to a 35 per cent rebate on the payment from the employer's Redundancy Fund!

INSURANCE

Both you and your nanny ought to be insured. You need insurance cover in case any accident happens to your nanny while she is working in your home. Suppose, for example, she slips on the mat in the hall and breaks her leg. Make sure that your household insurance policy would cover you against any claim. And, if she is to drive your car, you will obviously need to make certain that she is included on your car insurance.

It is perhaps not so obvious that your nanny should take out an insurance policy. But she might become involved in some incident which ends up in a claim against her. The classic example is the runaway buggy that she has accidentally let go down a hill; it runs directly into the road and causes a dreadful accident. Not very likely maybe – but for a small premium, such accidents *are* worth her insuring against. There are some companies that will offer insurance cover specially designed for nannies.

*

Redundancy and insurance claims are a sad place to end the formal side of employing a nanny. If you are just about to engage a nanny for the first time, they will seem very far from your thoughts. But in many ways the key to success in employing a nanny is always to be foreseeing the next stage of the game. The legal rules do provide some general framework for that foresight.

6

Finding a nanny: first thoughts to the advertisement

A NANNY OR NOT?

A good nanny is for most people the ideal form of childcare. She will be based in your own home – so you will not have to struggle to get your kids dressed and out to the nursery or childminder before you get to work yourself. She will take charge of buying the essential supplies, nappies, baby wipes, disinfectant and so forth – so you will not have to spend your weekends on one mad shopping expedition. She will be able to work flexible hours – so you will be able to fit in some late evenings at work or early starts. She will adapt her routine to the changing needs of the kids, nursing them if they are sick, arranging outings to friends and to a variety of entertainments. She will be expensive, but probably not as outlandishly expensive as you might imagine. If you have two children under five, a nanny may well be a cheaper form of childcare than two full-time places at a good private day nursery.

It all *sounds* marvellous. If you can afford it and if you can find a *good* nanny, it really can solve most of your problems. But there is another side. Things can go wrong. Sometimes this can be dramatic. We have all heard the stories of the mother who returns from work unexpectedly at midday – to find the nanny with her feet up in front of the telly and the kids playing with matches in the kitchen. But the trouble is normally much more mundane – illness and unpunctuality. You may think it wonderfully convenient to be able to leave your children at home with the nanny when they would be too ill to take to the nursery or childminder. Of course it is. But remember – nannies sometimes get ill too; and some get ill more often than others. You may begin to see the advantages of a day nursery after your nanny has been laid up for weeks with tonsilitis, followed by flu, followed by a nasty bout of food poisoning. And you may curse the train service that regularly lands her on your doorstep a good twenty minutes late. Not only this – but your nanny will, in the end, leave. If you are lucky, this will be planned well in advance. But some nannies do walk out overnight – leaving you in the lurch and the kids confused and upset.

On balance, those of us who can afford nannies at home have the easiest form of childcare – when it works. But it needs careful planning and a degree of luck. For some people childminders or day nurseries (see Chapters 9 and 10) will seem a better bet, and not just because they are cheaper.

BEFORE YOU START

Suppose you have decided to employ a nanny. Don't rush. Don't put an advert in your local paper straight away. Don't race round to the nearest employment agency. Think first about what your needs will be, what kind of employment you can offer, and what *style* of nanny is likely to suit you best. Admittedly, at the outset some of these issues will feel a bit abstract – especially if this is the first time you have employed a nanny and (even more so) if you do not yet have a baby. But it does help to be as clued up as possible about different types of arrangement *before* you get embroiled in the practicalities of advertising and interviewing. If it all seems too remote, try talking to friends who have a nanny or (better still) their nanny herself. It is a good idea to try to see things from the nanny's point of view from the very beginning.

Live-in or live-out

For most people the biggest question is whether their nanny will come in daily or 'live-in', at least during the week. There is no perfect solution here – but advantages and disadvantages on either side.

Expense

If your nanny lives in, she will *seem* cheaper. You will pay her less, if you are providing her with free board and lodging. But the saving can be a bit illusory. She will, after all, use heat, light, electricity and the telephone. You may choose to ask her for a contribution towards her phone calls. But do not imagine that you will get the full cost back. It is simply human nature to *under*estimate the length of a phone call. And your nanny will be in the house on her own for much of the day. What would *you* do in her position, on her salary? There are also considerable 'start-up' costs in employing a live-in nanny. She will normally expect to have her own television in her room. And you may find that your old spare bed is not really good enough for someone to sleep on regularly...

Punctuality and privacy

If she lives in, she will be on hand for more flexible hours. There will be no problem about lateness in the morning (unless she is an enormously heavy sleeper) and evening babysitting will be much easier to arrange. On the other hand, you will lose a spare room in your house and a lot of privacy. And you will be dealing with an extra 'body' around the place whose habits you will not know until she has been with you a few weeks. She might be a sheer delight to live with. But she might want to spend an hour in your only bathroom every morning or play aggressively loud music at your quiet times.

Part of the family?

A live-in nanny will more quickly become 'part of the family'. This can seem much more friendly – and nice for the kids, who will see their day-time carer side by side with their mother. But there are disadvantages both for you and for the nanny. For the nanny, it will mean that she is never really off duty. You may know that she does not work after six o'clock – but your toddler will not be able to tell the difference between the working and non-working day. There will be demands for a story or help with a jigsaw from the nanny at any hour of the day or night. And the nanny, in practice, will find it hard to resist. From *your* point of view, having a nanny as part of the family will make it much more difficult ever to treat her as an 'employee'. Maybe that will never be necessary. Maybe your views on childcare will always coincide with hers. But if you *do* need to say 'Do it my way, not yours' you will find it much more difficult if everyone is just one big happy family. Don't be too sentimental. A family atmosphere can make giving orders next to impossible.

A live-out nanny will often find it easier to feel 'professional' about her job. She will look after your kids during the day. In the evenings and at weekends she can escape from the irritations of your family and live her own life. The troubles of Monday will not necessarily spill over to Monday evening and Tuesday. And for this reason alone, she is likely to stay with you longer. Don't forget nannying is only a job. To *you* your kids are the most precious things in the world, and you hope that they will become precious to your nanny too. But in the end, she is bound to leave and look after others. It may be best to encourage the slight sense of detachment that comes with living out and to treat your nanny as an employed, professional, loving childcarer, not a substitute Mother or Auntie. But, of course, that detachment also has its inconvenient sides – simply in practical terms. Even the very best nanny will occasionally be late (can you honestly say that *you* have never been late for work?) and she is likely to find evening work much less to her taste.

To sum up

Some mothers will have no choice on the question of live-in or live-out. If you have no spare room of a decent size, then you will have to opt for a daily nanny. If, on the other hand, you are rich enough to have a house with a self-contained flat (a 'nanny wing'!), then you can have the best of both worlds – the advantages of a nanny on the spot, *and* of your own (and her) privacy. For most of us, it is best to be aware of the advantages and disadvantages on either side but not make a *final* decision until we have started interviewing. You may *think* you want a nanny to live out, but find that the only girl you really like wants a live-in job. Remember too that there are some compromise positions. Some live-in nannies make a point of going away every weekend – which may give you enough time on your own, as a family. And some daily nannies are prepared to stay overnight on occasion, if you need late-night (or even all-night) cover from time to time. So, be aware of the different options, but try not to be too rigid.

Your 'style' of nanny

There are many kinds of nanny, and many kinds of nanny jobs. Before you advertise or approach an agency, there are some decisions you must make. What sort of job is it that you are offering? Are there any groups of people (smokers, for example, or non-drivers) that you will never want to consider for the job? Again do not be too precise. If you construct too detailed a picture of your 'perfect nanny' (twenty-three, Princess Christian trained, social smoker, dog lover, experienced with tiny babies), you run a major risk of never finding her – and of passing over some very good candidates in the process. But if you *know* that you could never bear to share your house with a smoker, you might as well be clear about that from the very beginning.

Domestic work

Will you want your nanny to do any domestic work apart from looking after your children? If the answer is 'yes', you may have a problem. Most trained nannies are reluctant to take on any housework – apart from what is directly related to the child. Is the housework really important to you? Do you want the nanny to give priority to the cleaning above what she might do with the children? Of course, when the baby is four months old and sleeping for three hours of the working day, even the highest class nanny might take to some dusting just to relieve the boredom! But an active toddler can provide a good day's work for the best nanny. If you are quite certain that you do want some cleaning done, you should advertise for a 'nanny/mother's help' (see p. 71). This will normally attract the untrained, but experienced nanny, who will often expect to do a bit of housework.

Driving

Will it be essential that your nanny can drive? Be realistic. You cannot expect your nanny to stay at home on her own, with just a few trips on foot to the local park and shops. You will want her to socialise and to meet others with young kids – and that will almost always be easier by car. Besides, you will also want her to be quickly mobile in case of emergencies. This is not a problem only for those in the remote countryside. Unless you live close to the centre of a friendly town and have only one child, you will find that a car driver is *highly desirable*. Whose car she drives is, of course, another question. But if the nanny does not own a car herself, you will probably end up giving her the use of yours – even at the cost of going to work by bike yourself!

Personal qualities

What personal qualities are going to be most important to you? Smoking is one obvious issue here – but try to think a little more widely. How does your household work? What are your main interests? If you are convinced and practising Christians, whose life revolves around the local church, it would be crazy to engage a nanny (particularly a live-in one) who did not share your faith. Or again, if you and your partner spend your every spare minute breeding and training a large family of Siamese cats, you will have to find a nanny who is a cat lover – or who, at the very least, is prepared to tolerate their constant presence. Age is another factor. For some people, a middle-aged woman – probably untrained, but with the experience of bringing up her own kids – makes the ideal daily nanny. Others cannot face the thought of establishing their own routines with a nanny almost twice their age who has 'seen it all before'. Too much like hiring your own mother to look after the kids! All these preferences will, of course, differ from person to person and family to family. On most things you will probably be prepared to compromise – happily tolerating your madly carnivorous nanny in a strictly vegetarian household! But do try to be aware at the very beginning what you will *not* compromise on.

Pay

What can you afford to pay your nanny? Wages differ a lot from area to area. You need to find out the going rate for where you live. The best way to do this is to talk to friends who have nannies, and to some nannies themselves (who have, predictably, the acutest view of all on what is a decent wage!). If you can't manage this, try talking to a local employment agency. Or even (more sneakily) ring up a few advertisements for nannies in your local paper. Pretend to be interested in the job and ask what the salary is. You will quickly get an idea of the normal range of wages. But remember that all kinds of other factors will come into play when you fix the exact salary. You can expect to pay a little less for a girl straight from college or untrained, a little more for a trained NNEB with several years' experience. You will pay more if she is looking after more than one child – though no nanny expects anything like a double salary for looking after two. You will pay more for longer hours, a little less if you can guarantee a relatively short, regular working week. Remember also to count in the expense of tax and National Insurance (see Chapter 5). Many nannies, when they tell you what they earn, think in terms of *take home* pay. As a rough guide, you should add 30 per cent to that figure to get the real cost to you.

opefully eager) nanny is going to get bored.

If it is really important to you to have trained help on har
e minute the baby is born, you may be better off arrangir
r a temporary 'maternity nurse', before your permane
nny starts. Maternity nurses specialise in short-term care
other and new-born baby, and they are quite used to a
ratic timetable – and to babies not arriving when the
ould! They live in and will often provide almost twenty-fou
our cover for things like nappy changing, bathing, winding
tc. Go to an agency if you are interested in this kind o
rrangement. Maternity nurses are not usually hired through
ewspaper adverts.

Where to advertise

The largest collection of advertisements for nannying jobs
appears in *The Lady* magazine. Buried among articles on
hire horses and Victorian flower painters are literally
hundreds of adverts for all kinds of domestic help – from
butlers to granny-sitters. Most nannies who are seriously
interested in finding a new job look in here. So you can pretty
well guarantee that any reasonable advert will bring some
response.

There are some snags though. First of all, *The Lady* appears
weekly and will not accept adverts by phone. You have to get
your text to them by first post on Wednesday for it to appear
the following Wednesday or Thursday. So, unless you time it
exactly right, you will have a gap of nearly a fortnight
between writing your advert and seeing it appear – an
inconvenient delay if you are in a hurry.

Second, you are liable to get replies from all over the
country. This may cause a problem when it comes to
interviewing. Are you going to pay the expenses for a
reasonable sounding applicant to come down from
Edinburgh or across from Taunton? You can hardly expect
the nanny to pay it all herself – but it could add a lot of money
to the cost of filling your job. It is probably not much to worry
about if you live in London (because enough of your
applicants will come from London anyway), or if you live in

Don't try to employ a nanny on the cheap. If you offer less
pay than the going rate, the chances are that you will get
someone unable to find a better job. The chances are too that
she will demand a hefty pay rise after a few weeks – and you
will either have to give in, or go through the inconvenience,
expense and upset for your child of finding a replacement.
Nannies may not be as expensive as you might think. But
unless you can afford the going rate, can give at least small
pay rises at reasonable intervals and still have enough left to
pay for the incidental expenses of employing a nanny (more
food, extra insurance on the car, etc), then you ought to think
first about cheaper alternatives – a childminder or (if you have
just one or maybe two children) a day nursery.

To sum up

The best advice at this stage is – be realistic and be as flexible
as possible. If you have pots of money and an enormous
house, you will be able to hire any kind of nanny you want – a
'traditional nanny' perhaps, with a little brown uniform and all
the trimmings! Most people should put that image right out of
their heads. The vast majority of nannies wear jeans and a
sweatshirt. And they are no better or worse at their job for
that. Think carefully about what *your* job will entail. The first
priority will be to get someone who will give excellent care to
the kids. A close second (very close, if she is to live in) will be
someone who can work easily with the *whole* family. After
that try to keep an open mind.

ADVERTS AND AGENCIES

There are two main ways of finding a nanny – advertising in
the local or national press; or using an employment agency
(normally a specialist agency for nannies and other domestic
help).

If you need someone urgently, you are probably best
advised to place a couple of adverts and at the same time to
register with a selection of agencies. This is a relatively
expensive procedure. But most agencies ask for only a small

fee to register, keeping their main charge for when you engage someone through them. So it probably won't be *prohibitively* expensive. The greater risk is that you will be bombarded with applicants at all hours of the day or night. But if you are really desperate, this will be a small price to pay.

If you have more time on your hands, you could use a different strategy. If, for example, you have not yet returned to work and are looking for someone several months in advance, it is worth trying a few adverts first. This is overall the cheapest way of finding someone – and if it works, so much the better. If it doesn't, you will still have time to go through some agencies. But do remember that it may take you several weeks to decide that your advert has drawn a blank. Don't leave your approach to the agencies too late if you have a deadline.

When to advertise

Everything will take longer than you think. You will need to allow a *minimum of two months* from the time you write your advert to the time you can expect the nanny to start. That may sound ridiculously long. But it could take up to two weeks to get your advert published. You will then need another two weeks to see the applicants, take up references and make up your mind. Then your chosen nanny will probably have to work out a month's notice in her current job. That makes two months. Of course, it *could* go quicker. You might get your advert into the local paper tomorrow. You might like the very first girl you see. And she might have only one week's notice to work. Total time – two weeks. But the chances are that it will take *even longer* than two months. Your first advert may bring a poor response and you end up placing another one, with yet more delay. You might find that it takes longer than you think to follow up references. Your first choice candidate might actually turn the job down. Or she might have promised her current employers that she would give them six weeks' notice. It is not in your interests to upset that kind of arrangement. After all, you will want her to work out her notice scrupulously when she comes to leave *you*.

There are nannies looking for jobs at all times of the year.

But when you choose to advertise *can* make a ⌐ number and quality of the applicants. If you are newly trained NNEB, remember that they finish the summer and are usually looking to start about July and September. The best time to adv their attention is the late spring or early summ should send a copy of your ad to the NNEB cours local technical college or college of further ed NNEB can provide you with a list of all colleges the NNEB exam.)

The worst period for trying to find a nanny Christmas. It is much better to advertise for some early January than mid-December. And it is better to place your advert until early in the new yea afford to be that flexible. The reason for this is people do not normally choose to disrupt their Christmas time, particularly in 'family-based' jobs.

A first baby: when to advertise

There are particular problems in deciding when t for a nanny for your first baby. It can seem like te to place an advert *before* the baby is born. But yo to do that unless you are intending to take several work after the birth. Be quite blunt with the appl interview. Remind them that you cannot *guarant* live, perfect, healthy baby. Unless they react sensi suggestion and seem prepared to take on the chall sick child then steer well clear of them.

On the other hand, do not plan *too* far in advan end up with a very long overlap period – while you home full-time *and* your nanny is already worki nannies like to have a week or so to get to know the around the house and your general ideas for the bal they like to be able to get on with the job without y constantly there. Be particularly careful that you don' with a nanny working for you before the baby has Not only is it a waste of money, but there is no job and, if it drags on for more than a week or so, yo

such a remote place that pretty well *any* applicant is going to have miles to travel. But for many people it may be more convenient to try and tap the *local* market first.

Nursery World

You will meet the same problems if you advertise in *Nursery World*. This is almost the trade magazine of the professional nanny. It carries articles on the practice and politics of childcare, as well as adverts for nursery nurses in schools and hospitals and for family nannies. Quite a different image from *The Lady*. But unfortunately it only appears once a fortnight on a Thursday – and you have to get your advert in (by phone, if you want) by the preceding Friday. This could mean a delay of three weeks between deciding on your advert and getting it published.

The local paper

In many cases the best place to advertise may be the local evening or weekly paper. You will generally find almost no delay in getting the advert published and you will attract a largely local response. This means no problems with interviewing – and there are other advantages too. If you are looking for a daily nanny, you will almost certainly want someone already living locally. And even if you are intending to employ a live-in nanny, it is a help to have someone who already knows your area. This is not only (or even mainly) for the sake of your kids – but also for the sake of your nanny. She will settle into the job much quicker if she has doesn't have to start a new social life from scratch.

On the practical side, take advantage of any special offers in your local evening paper – four nights for the price of three, for example. Not everyone looks at the paper every night. And make sure that one of your nights is a Saturday. This will catch people coming to your area at weekends because they particularly want to move there, or move back there. Always check too that the paper does carry other adverts for nannies, if only a handful. If there are *no* others, you would be better off using *The Lady* or *Nursery World*. Nannies will not look in the paper if they don't expect to find jobs there.

How not to write an advert

Urgent! Gemma (4) and Tristram (11 months – and a bundle of energy!) want a super nanny to look after them in busy, chaotic house in Hampstead. Fun job. Loving personality and sense of humour more important than paper qualifications. Ring 01 485 1000.

Many mothers write adverts like this – to try to make *their* job sound interesting, amusing and a bit different from the ordinary. But stop a minute and think how it must sound to a prospective nanny.

The advert goes wrong from the very first word. What sort of person can fill an *urgent* vacancy? Probably not the sort you particularly want to apply. Not those currently in a nannying job, intending to make a move after working out their full period of notice – but those without work, or those who are prepared to leave their present employers at the drop of a hat. Some of these may, of course, make excellent nannies, but they are certainly not the safest end of the market! Worse than this, *why* is the job so 'urgent'? Even to a pretty naive reader it looks as if Gemma and Tristram's previous nanny might have left in a bit of a hurry. The single word 'urgent' suggests that there might be more to this than meets the eye.

The second sentence is not much better. It conjures up visions of doting parents and exceedingly tiresome children. His mum might think little Tristram is a 'bundle of energy' – but that does look suspiciously like a euphemism for 'pain in the neck'. And what about this busy and chaotic house? Are mum and dad going to be *so* busy that they are never quite home on time? *You* might think disorder is rather cute, but a nanny might think that it is simply another word for exploitation.

Worst of all is the jibe about the nanny's qualifications. Trained nannies have normally done a two-year course in childcare and development, followed by a set of formal exams. They are not going to take kindly to an employer who claims to rate proper professional qualifications lower than such woolly qualities as a 'loving personality'. You may want to *encourage* untrained girls to apply. But don't do it in such a way that positively *discourages* the trained applicants.

A final word of warning. It can be dangerous to give your children's names in an advert if you also give your phone number. Nuisance callers have been known to look through such adverts and even to bother children. The danger is very remote. But if you *must* give your kids' names and you want to be absolutely safe, then you will have to use a box number. Though this will mean that your applicants will have to *write* to you and the whole process will take a lot longer.

Nanny required (NNEB preferred) for two boys in Georgian house in pretty part of Bristol. Live-in. Own room (newly decorated and washbasin). Salary £100 per week. Possibility of family holidays to France and Austria. Must be responsible. References essential. Write to Mrs J. Smith, 26 Beauvoir Terrace, Clifton, Bristol.

This advert is not as bad as the last one. But it wastes words (and money) talking about unimportant, possibly misleading, details. And it misses out basic, essential information.

The biggest error here is to state the salary. Obviously *you* must have an upper limit in mind. But why commit yourself to paying this, when you might find an excellent nanny just out of college, who would happily do the job for less? And why put off those who are looking for a slightly higher salary? For the sake of getting someone really good, you probably would be prepared to pay five or ten pounds more a week. Besides, what does '£100' mean? Is it gross salary or take-home pay (see pp. 75, 112)? And for how many hours a week? It makes a bit of a difference whether it covers a standard forty-hour week or something approaching sixty hours and every other weekend! Stated baldly in an advert, without explanation, a salary figure will almost certainly mislead.

It is also a mistake to go on at such length about the 'fringe benefits'. You are trying to attract someone who wants to look after your kids, not an enthusiast for Georgian architecture or a keen traveller! Besides, the perks mentioned are not exactly that wonderful – as nanny perks go. It is all very well to point out that you can offer a self-contained flat. That really might attract a whole different range of applicants. But new decoration and a wash basin are nothing very special. So don't make yourself look ridiculous by *overselling* the job.

The most glaring omission is the age of the boys. For most nannies this advert is next to useless, because they have no way of telling whether the kids are 2 and 4 or 11 and 14. Different ages make for quite different jobs. And different nannies have different preferences – although *most* would choose to look after babies and young kids rather than 'mind' a couple of difficult adolescents after school and during the holidays! Don't waste your money on stating the obvious ('Must be responsible', 'References essential') and forget the really crucial information.

There are some advantages in asking your applicants to *write* rather than phone. It tends to put off those who aren't very serious anyway. It gives you more time to decide on who to interview – useful if you are bad at making quick decisions on the telephone. And letters can be a much safer guide to the quality of the applicant than a nervous and hasty phone call. But do remember that the phone is a much quicker way of conducting the whole business. If you are in a hurry to find someone, don't suggest that your applicants *write* to you.

The right way to write an advert

Try to put yourself in the position of a nanny reading your advert. What information *must* she have before she can decide to apply for the job? Think of this first. Are you looking for someone with specific qualifications (such as the NNEB)? Is the job for a live-in or a daily nanny? Or doesn't it matter? How many kids are there? And how old are they? Are there any skills (such as driving) that you particularly want your nanny to have? Is there anything that she needs to know *in advance* about your home and family?

Don't ask for particular personal qualities. There is no sense in advertising for a nanny who is 'caring and loving'. After all, every potential nanny will *think* herself caring and loving. It will be up to you at interview to decide whether or not she really is. The same goes for 'responsible'. If what you mean by asking for someone 'responsible' is that they will have to take sole charge of the children, then say this. Many nannies prefer jobs where they will not constantly be under the parents' feet.

Don't say too much about the perks. Most good nannies are pretty down to earth about these things and won't be attracted by vague promises of trips abroad. But do make it clear if you can offer *self-contained* accommodation to a live-in nanny. Some nannies would only consider a live-in job if they could have their own place to escape to.

Think also about your own convenience. Decide whether you would prefer your applicants to phone or to write – or even to write to a box number, if you want to stay completely anonymous. If you ask people to phone, then make sure you state the time of day they should call. It is pretty nerve racking to sit at home waiting for applicants to ring. You rush to the phone after hours of silence, all ready with your 'nanny questions' – only to find that it is your mother! Or you get so driven to distraction by applicants phoning all day long that you end up taking it off the hook! You will save your nerves a lot of strain if you firmly state that people should ring between 7 and 9 – or whatever times are most convenient to you. Just remember that some nannies will find it difficult to call about a new job in their normal working hours. So don't make it between 1 and 3 in the afternoon.

The following adverts give you some idea of good, concise wording.

NNEB, or equivalent, for two boys (18 months and 3). Cambridge. Live-in, own room. Non-smoker, driver essential. Phone 0223 912734, 6-8 pm.

This is about as short an advert as you can reasonably get, but it contains all the necessary information for a standard job. It asks in the first instance for a *qualified* nanny. But by saying 'or equivalent' it doesn't exclude an untrained girl with experience. The phrase 'own room' is the usual formula for the minimum of accommodation you might offer a nanny – a bedsit, sharing a bathroom with the family. No starting date is mentioned. This will normally be taken to mean that you want a nanny as soon as is reasonably possible, but not *urgently*.

Nanny required from January, Islington. 21+. NNEB preferred. Live in or out. Girl (1), boy (4, at nursery mornings). Parents doctor and dentist. Sole charge. Must be non-smoker, driver (car provided) and cat-lover! Domestic help employed. Phone 01-226-1010. 7-9 pm.

This advert gives more information and is a bit more precise in its requirements.

'Sole charge' makes it absolutely clear that the nanny will be on her own looking after one of the children all day, and both in the afternoons. She will also presumably collect the older child from his nursery school. 'Domestic help employed' adds nothing very specific – but does underline the fact that the nanny's job will be entirely childcare and no cleaning! This will appeal to a lot of professional nannies.

Stating the parents' occupations can help a potential applicant decide whether it is her kind of job. An experienced nanny will know that it is one thing to work for a family of actors, with their obviously erratic hours – quite another to work for teachers, who are likely to be based at home (and under her feet!) for much of the school holidays. If it is likely to give a nanny some idea of the 'style' of your family, then say in your advert what your own line of work is.

To demand a cat-lover is a fair warning that the house will be overrun by precious Siamese! Most nannies are happy to take a family tabby in their stride. But anything much more than that needs to be advertised in advance – unless a lot of time is to be wasted interviewing girls who feel queasy at the smell of trays of cat food. The same goes, of course, for dogs, horses, goats or any other particular passion of the family.

What an agency can do for you – and the cost

If you use an employment agency, you will save yourself the trouble of writing and placing an advert. But you might not save yourself much more.

Some agencies simply provide you with a list and brief details of girls available on their books – and you then get in touch with them directly. Or alternatively the nannies, who are given details of *your* requirements by the agency, get in touch with you. The advantage of such an agency is that you can sit down with your list straight away and look over a wide range of potential nannies. You won't have to wait until they see your advert and ring you, one by one. You can also be fairly sure (if you have chosen a reputable agency) that the nannies are who they say they are. The agency should have checked out their references and have eliminated any obvious frauds. The disadvantage is that you then have to make contact with them. They may be difficult to get hold of. And when finally you do, you may find that they have already accepted a job elsewhere – often through a newspaper advert or another agency. Meanwhile other nannies who have been given your number by the agency *may* be trying independently to get in contact with you. It can all seem rather more out of your control than an advert in the local paper.

Other agencies offer a fuller service. They will take the details of your requirements and try to match these up to the girls on their books. They will then present you with a 'short list' of nannies to interview. This takes much more of the load off you. But you do need to trust your agency. You need to be certain that they have really understood what kind of a nanny you are looking for. And, even more important, you must be sure that they have enough nannies registered with them to have a reasonable choice in making their shortlist. Otherwise their 'selection' doesn't mean very much.

All agencies should be able to give you advice on rates of pay and conditions of employment. They should have a good idea of the going rate for your kind of job, the amount of holiday expected, and so on. They might even be able to provide model contracts for you to use.

No agency can take over the responsibility of being an employer. You will have to interview all the shortlisted nannies yourself (and normally pay at least part of their interview expenses). And you will have to recheck the references of the successful applicant yourself (see pp. 135-7). The agency should already have followed up the previous employers. But they will take no responsibility for any mistakes or misrepresentations. You must do this before finally offering the job.

Agency fees vary tremendously. But, as a rough guide, the more services they offer, the more expensive they will be. The top London agencies may charge as much as 10 per cent of the nanny's annual salary when you engage someone through them – though many other agencies will be quite a lot cheaper. It may seem over-priced, compared with a simple ad in the local paper. But remember, after a small initial registration charge, you will only pay the main fee if you actually engage someone through the agency. And if the arrangement breaks down within the first weeks, the agency will normally try to provide a replacement for no extra fee. If you end up with an excellent nanny who stays with you for two or three years, you may feel that the apparently hefty fee was well worth it.

Reasons for using an agency

You may feel happier using an agency rather than advertising by yourself. It puts a middleman between you and the quite unfamiliar world of nannies, their qualifications, salaries, rights and expectations. A good agency has experience of that world – and should prevent the kind of disaster that can arise if you are completely naive about what makes a competent nanny.

But there are other particular reasons for using an agency instead of, or as well as, advertising.

- If you need to find a nanny quickly, you will have to use an agency *as well* as advertising. To attract a reasonable number of applicants in a very short time, you can't afford to leave any method untried.
- If you live in London, you may find an agency a more efficient way of discovering a good nanny. There are too

many local papers in the capital to be sure of an advert in just one of them reaching the right audience. And nannies in London tend to rely rather more on agencies for finding work than those outside.

- If you have very special requirements, it is probably best to use an agency. There is, for example, one agency that *specialises* in nannies for the handicapped. And most agencies ask their nannies in advance whether they would be willing to work with a handicapped child. In general, agencies may be better than a simple advert at finding a nanny who is prepared to work in a very remote place or very unusual hours.
- If you need someone temporarily, then it will not be worth your while to advertise. Many agencies have staff on their books who are looking for temporary work. And they will charge you a lower fee for finding a 'temp' rather than a permanent nanny.
- If you are convinced that you only want a Norland nanny, you should use the Norland Register, which is the Training College itself operating as an agency for its own trainees. Though in practice you *can* find Norland nannies registered with other agencies.

How to choose an agency

Be realistic about agencies. They are not *charities* set up to make the life of the working mother easier. They make money out of *you* when they find you a nanny you will employ. They do not charge the nanny anything for finding her a job. There is a pressure to deception here on both sides. *You* will try and make your job sound as attractive as possible – more attractive than it really is. The *agency* will try and make its nannies sound as well qualified and as well suited to you as possible. Nobody is actually lying. They are just making the best of the perfectly ordinary job they are offering – or of the perfectly ordinary girls they have on their books. Remember this when some charming lady assures you on the telephone that she has 'just the nanny for you'. That charming lady won't make any money unless you decide to engage that particular nanny, or one of the others she can offer you!

You will find a large number of advertisements for nanny agencies in *The Lady*. And your local yellow pages will probably carry some under the heading 'Employment Agencies'. First sift through these. Note down any that advertise any of the special things you might be interested in – temporary nannies, for example, maternity nurses, nannies for the handicapped. And if you are looking for a daily nanny, note particularly any agencies near your home. Then ask around your friends. Find out if any of them have used an agency that they would recommend. Word of mouth can be the best way of finding a good agency. But remember that people often recommend an agency just because they found *one* good nanny through them. That could have been luck – the right nanny at the right time. It certainly does not guarantee that they will find *you* someone good – or even that the service is thorough or efficient.

Then start ringing around a few agencies. Tell them roughly what you are looking for and ask them to send you details of their agency and registration forms. But ask some important questions at this point.

- Find out how many nannies they have placed in the last year. If they are *very* reticent about this, beware.
- Ask whether they themselves have interviewed all the nannies they have on their books. Good agencies will try to do this for all nannies registering, unless it is really impossible (if the nanny lives abroad, for example). Don't trust those agencies that have only asked the nanny to supply references and fill in a questionnaire. These questionnaires are not usually very revealing. They simply ask for a few basic facts about the nanny's health, qualifications, experience, likes and dislikes ('Do you have diabetes?', 'Can you swim?', 'Do you cook?', and so on). One agency even suggested to my own nanny that an attractive photograph would be the most important thing for getting her a good job. Maybe that is true – but if so, it is frightening!
- Ask whether they provide you with a complete list of nannies available, or whether they pre-select a shortlist.

You may prefer either system. But you certainly need to know which you will be getting.

- Find out if the agency is a member of the Federation of Recruitment and Employment Services (FRES). Members of this organisation operate within a clear and sensible code of practice, designed to protect nanny and employer alike. They have a lot of experience in the private nanny market and even have a seat on the board of the NNEB – representing the interests of employers in the private sector. There are perfectly reputable agencies outside the FRES, but (if you know nothing else about them) membership of the Federation does give you some guarantee of proper minimum standards.

You will have to make up your mind pretty quickly which agencies to choose and how many. Their registration details, their fees and the answers to your questions should narrow the choice down a lot. But should you use just one agency or several? In an ideal world, you would choose just one. You would get to know them well, so that they understood exactly what kind of nanny would suit you – and you would go back to them each time you needed somebody new. That *can* still work. But if you are in a hurry and you have not actually used an agency before, it is probably better to register with two or three. That way you don't risk being taken in by an agency that sounds very plausible, but can't actually produce the goods.

*

Once the agency has produced its full list or its shortlist, you will be *on your own*, just as if you had advertised yourself. It will be up to you to decide which nanny you could work with best. It will be up to you to (re)check her references. The next chapter on interviewing is written mostly with the private advertiser in mind. But (although some agencies will do some of the work for you) most of the advice applies to the agency-user as well.

7

Finding a nanny: the interview and after

Once you have got your short-list, *don't rush*. You will obviously want to find a nanny as quickly as possible. But you can't afford to go through the whole business so quickly that you make avoidable mistakes. There are three stages in the process. First the *initial phone call* or *letter*. You will rule out some applicants at this point, because it will be immediately obvious that they do not meet any of your basic requirements. The next stage is the *first interview*. You should try to see a good number of applicants (at least seven or eight, if possible), to get an idea of what the field of talent is like. Then make up a final short list of two or three – and see these applicants for a *second interview* before you make up your mind.

BEFORE THE INTERVIEW

The first phone call or letter

The phone is the quickest way for your applicants to get in touch with you. But you need to be able to think on your feet. Keep a pencil and paper by the phone – as well as a list of all the questions you will want to ask and the things you need to tell anyone who phones. It is also useful to have a ready made out timetable of when you will be able to interview.

When someone rings:

- Take down her name, address and telephone number straight away.

- Check that she does meet the requirements of your advert. If, for example, you have asked for 'NNEB or experience', find out what experience she actually has. There are a few girls who think that occasional babysitting is good enough qualification for being a nanny. In this case you must say politely and firmly that there is no point in her coming for an interview.
- If she sounds promising, arrange a time for her to come to interview. If she lives locally, you should allow about half an hour – you can always bring her back. But if she is coming from a distance, allow at least 45 minutes (after all, you don't have to use all that time). Make clear at this stage whether or not you will contribute to her travel expenses for coming to interview.
- Don't forget to give her your address and clear directions on how to reach your house.
- If you get a really large number of calls (and it does sometimes happen), you will have to sift out the applicants rather more carefully on the telephone. After all, you won't be able to interview 50 nannies! Talk to each applicant about her last job, about the kind of post she is looking for now, about the salary she would expect and so on. Then ring her back (or write) when you have decided which you will be able to see.

You will follow the same kind of procedure if your applicants write to you. But you will have more time to think about each one and to study her letter of application. The basic rule here is to move on to the telephone as quickly as possible after the first written approach. Otherwise it will take you literally weeks to get to see the applicants. If her letter gives a phone number, then ring up to arrange an interview. If it does not, offer her an interview in writing – but ask her to confirm by phone.

Preparing for the interviews

Before the interviews, you will need to think more carefully about the details of your job. What will the exact duties be?

Will the nanny have to collect the older kids from school? How many days holiday will she get? What will the normal hours of work be? You won't have to have absolutely everything worked out in advance. Some things will be agreed later with whoever you choose to appoint. But the nanny is bound to ask questions at the interview – and you can't simply say 'We'll have to decide that later' in response to *every* question.

If you plan to have a live-in nanny, you will need to decide what room (or rooms) she will have – and what the furniture and other equipment will be. You must show the nanny her accommodation at the first interview. It is no good parading a large room with double bed and colour TV, if you end up giving her a tiny attic (with a single bed and black-and-white TV).

You must also decide who is going to handle the interview. You and your partner will probably both want to be there and ask questions. But you must know in advance which of you is going to answer the nanny's queries, and who is going to decide when to show the nanny round the house or when to bring things to a close. Another issue is whether your children are going to be around. If you have just a tiny baby, it is a good idea to have him at the interview. You will, after all, want to see how she handles the baby. But if your kids are old enough to know what is going on, you may decide to spare them this first stage – though you must involve them when you have a shortlist.

THE INTERVIEW

If you are not used to interviewing, you will find it more difficult than you think to discover the important information about your candidates. The commonest mistake is to talk too much yourself. You may well enjoy the experience – chatting about your kids and your job. But you won't find out much about your potential nannies.

The first interview has two functions. *You* have to decide whether the applicant is possible for your job. *She* has to decide whether it is the kind of job she wants. Some of this will be instinctive. You may know from the minute she walks in the door that she could never be the nanny for you. But it is often not so simple. You may find some of the ideas that follow useful – though don't imagine that you have to use them all at one session!

Finding out about the nanny

- Ask her about her last job. What did she like about it? What did she dislike? How long did she stay and why is she leaving? If she has only just qualified, then ask her about the 'placements' she did at college. You will often get further by exploring her *dislikes*. It is less familiar ground, so you will get less prepared answers.
- Try not to ask leading questions or questions that encourage one word answers. To say 'You don't approve of corporal punishment, do you' is next to useless. If you want to find out what her attitudes to punishment are, you must be more open-ended. It would be much better to ask something like – 'Suppose our three-year-old had just deliberately hit the baby on the head with the hobbyhorse. What would you do?'
- Find out what her idea of daily activities might be. Look for someone with lots of initiative – not someone who says 'Well, we could go to the park, I suppose'. But don't be over-impressed by a long list of swimming, toddler club, duck-feeding, swings, zoo, Punch and Judy, and so forth. Find out what she *actually* does in her current job.
- Remember that your children will get older. Don't relate all your questions to a tiny baby. In a few months' time he will be a rough toddler – and you will need to get some idea of how she will cope then. Unfortunately, there *are* nannies who are wonderful at caring for little babies (who sleep most of the day anyway), but have not much clue about how to handle (or stimulate) a kid with all the demands of a two-year-old. Watch out for this.
- Ask her what she would *like* to be doing in ten years' time. This is a difficult question to answer (what would *you* say?). But nine times out of ten it is much more revealing than

asking, for example, if she intends to stay in nannying permanently. Don't be put off if she has ambitions to be doing something rather different in ten years' time. Some of the very best nannies use the job as a staging post to further training in nursing or teaching. But you might feel happier with someone who had considered plans to become a paediatric nurse, rather than wild fantasies about being a film actress!

- Check carefully *again* whether she meets the terms of your advert. The last time I advertised for a 'non-smoker', a good half of the applicants I interviewed reeked of tobacco. Maybe they would not have actually smoked in the house. But how could you know what they would have done when they went out, or to visit friends? If you want to be fairly certain that your children won't be smoked over, ask again (and explicitly) at the interview.

- Ask her how long she would intend to stay in the job. Don't expect her to volunteer the next five years of her life to you. If she does, she is probably lying. But you should be suspicious of someone who is not thinking in terms of *at least* a year. You will probably be curious about whether she is intending to get married or pregnant. But do try to avoid asking directly the kind of questions no one would ask a man – and which would infuriate you if *you* were asked them at a job interview!

- If you are interviewing a live-out nanny, ask carefully about how she intends to get to work. If she is likely to come by public transport, you must check that that is feasible before you take her on. You will only be making problems for yourself if you engage someone who is entirely dependent on one infrequent and unreliable bus. If she intends to drive, check on the state of her car! You don't want it to let her down once a week – nor do you want it to be a death trap for your kids, who will almost certainly be transported in it from time to time.

- Give her plenty of opportunity to ask *you* questions. These can be pretty revealing of her general grasp on the job – and her interests within it. As a rule of thumb, I decided to have nothing more to do with anyone who asked me what brand of disposable nappies I used! (Though it did seem more reasonable to want to know whether I used terries or disposables!)

Letting the nanny find out about you

Look at the areas covered by the specimen contracts (see pp. 98-100). You must touch on most of these at the first interview – even if a few points remain undecided.

- Before you talk about pay, make sure she knows what it is pay *for*. How many hours a week will she work? Will she be needed at weekends? What holiday entitlement will she have? Will she have any duties apart from care of the children? When it comes to naming a sum, you will have to think on your feet. You will already have a range in mind. But the exact sum will depend on the age, qualification and experience of the girl – and on what she expects. It is never worth turning down the best applicant, just because she wants £2 a week more than you had planned. Make it absolutely clear whether the figure you have named is before or after deductions of tax and National Insurance.
- Explain that you will provide a written contract of employment – and that, if she gets the job, you will discuss its terms with her before she has to sign.
- If you are interviewing a live-in nanny, discuss the living arrangements of the house. Will the nanny eat as part of the family? What if she wants to have friends round? What about overnight guests? Do you have any 'rules' – like 'no noise after midnight'? What will happen at weekends, if she is not working? Show her all over the house and point out carefully what is (and what is not) provided in her accommodation.
- Let her know your general preferences in childcare. Some of these will come out in the questions you put to her. But you can't grill her on absolutely everything. So make it clear, for example, that you don't like Radio One or the television on all day; that you try to feed the children a diet free of most added sugar; that you want your daughter

encouraged to play football and engineering games as well as sewing and 'nurses'. Don't make yourself sound completely rigid or 'faddy'. But remember it is *much* easier to raise these issues now than when she has already started the job.

- Try to think objectively about your job. Tell her the good things about it *and* the bad. I always make it clear to prospective nannies that both myself and my partner work from home quite a bit, that we sometimes want childcare into the evenings and that we do not pay 'showbiz' rates. And at our last round of interviews I warned them all that we were about to have the builders in for six months! I balance this gloomy picture by pointing out some of the nicer aspects of the job. No doubt some are still put off – but better at this point than later. If you are interviewing a first-time nanny, it is particularly important to stress how *lonely* the job can be. Most nannies are supervised most of the time during their training, and many do not realise how different, and isolating, it may turn out to be when they are *on their own* with a couple of toddlers for eight hours a day!

With some applicants you will know almost immediately that it is no good. Don't drag out the agony. Give them a short interview and, if you are brave enough, tell them on the spot that you will not be offering them the job. Alternatively (and this is what most of us do), write to them soon afterwards.

If you are very keen about the person you have interviewed, or even if you are uncertain, explain that you will be holding second interviews for a small shortlist of candidates. Say that you will be deciding on your shortlist when you have seen other applicants – and give some idea *how long* that is likely to take. Ask her to let you know (either immediately, or later) if she will *not* be interested in the job. And check again the best way of getting in touch with her quickly. You don't want to have a long delay once you have decided who to interview again. If you are absolutely certain after the first interview that you want someone on your shortlist, don't wait to get in touch with her later. Arrange a time for a second interview on the spot.

It is quite common to find that a few people do not show up for their interview. If they don't let you know in advance, then rule them out immediately – even if you are desperate, and even if they do ring up later with a plausible story. You may lose a very few good nannies by being tough like this. But you just can't risk relying on someone who doesn't even manage to turn up when they are supposed to be on their best behaviour!

REFERENCES

There are two attitudes to references. The first is to rely mostly on your own judgment about the applicants – and just to use the references at the very last stage, as a final check against disaster. The other is to use them, very positively, as one of the ways you make up your mind who to appoint.

If you want references just as a fail-safe device, then you don't need to bother about getting names until you have (at least in your own mind) decided who you want. If, on the other hand, you want references to help you choose between different applicants, then ideally you want to have been in touch with the referees before the final interview. At the first interview, ask all those who seem remotely possible to give you the name, address and phone number of two referees. You should normally insist that one of these is their current employer. Say that you won't get in touch with their referees unless you have decided to put the applicant on the final shortlist. Nobody wants their referees bothered about jobs that they only have the very remotest chance of getting.

You may find that some nannies do not want their present employers to be asked for a reference unless you actually intend to offer them the job. This usually means that they have not admitted that they are looking for a new job. There may be very good reasons for this. But it is a warning sign that they are not leaving their present job in the way that you would *hope* anyone would leave you.

A few nannies will not want to give their present employer as a referee at all. Again, this might be perfectly understandable. Some employers are utterly unreasonable and vindictive. And whatever has gone wrong in the job may not be the nanny's fault at all. But do check out the circumstances *very carefully*.

You must *always* try to talk to the referees on the phone. Begin with a letter if you like and get a written reference, but always follow it up with a phone call. For a start this tells you something about the referee. It will be obvious very quickly, for example, if he or she is just a friend of the nanny, who has used her for some babysitting. You should also be able to get some sense of the referee's judgment. Some people (and this includes some training course tutors anxious to find jobs for their nannies) are incapable of being critical about anyone.

When you talk to the referee on the phone, have a list of questions prepared. You may not need to use them, if the person you talk to is particularly helpful and forthcoming – but you want to be able to be business-like if necessary. Remember you can't expect a referee to have unlimited time to talk or be prepared to agonise with you about whether or not the girl is right for your job! But you will be able to check whether the image presented by the nanny is one recognised by her teachers or former employers. And you will be able to raise issues that are important to *you*, but which might be left out of a standard written reference.

These are some questions you might find useful. They will vary a bit, depending on whether you are talking to a former employer or to a training course tutor:

- What are the nanny's best qualities? What failings did she have, from their point of view? If the referee immediately comes out with a groan about hundreds of unwashed-up coffee cups and you are obsessively neat, then beware! But always remember that standards of tidiness vary. The unknown person you are talking to might herself be manically houseproud.
- What kind of activities did she do with the children? This is a good check on all the wonderful things the nanny might have promised at interview. If she didn't do them in her last job, she is unlikely to do them in yours.

- If you are talking to a course tutor, ask what placements the nanny did best on and what sort of job, in the tutor's opinion, she would be most suited to. Ask her to evaluate the student in relation to others in her year. This should reveal how well the tutor *actually* knows the girl, as well as breaking through the tutor's understandable desire to 'do the best' for each of her students.
- Is the nanny often ill and what is her *attitude* to illness? Obviously you are interested in her health and whether she suffers from any condition that might make it difficult for her to do your job. But just as important is to find out whether she is the sort who takes to her bed with every cold. It may sound tough – but you can't afford to have someone like that.
- What was she paid in her last job? Was she 'officially' employed, with tax and National Insurance paid? This will help you gauge the right salary level, if you haven't already fixed it. Remember a nanny is likely to exaggerate what she was getting in her last job (wouldn't you?). Or she may forget that she was just being paid cash – with all the future loss of benefits that that entails. It is important to know these details, though it can be a bit awkward to ask about them.
- Why did the nanny leave her last job – or why is she anxious to start a new one? Here again, it is useful to compare the nanny's story with the employer's. But don't fall into the trap of *automatically* believing the employer's version.
- Would the referee positively recommend the nanny for your job? You will need to give a thumbnail sketch of the kind of job you are offering and ask explicitly if he or she has any reservations at all about recommending the girl for such a post.

THE SECOND INTERVIEW

Only you can decide which of the nannies you want to put on your shortlist. But when you have narrowed it down to two or three (and any more would be much too time-consuming), arrange to see them again as quickly as possible. At this stage you will need to allow more time for each one. You must give the potential nanny at least an hour with your kids, so that each can get the measure of the other. And you must allow enough time for you all to discover how easily you can relate. If you have a trusted and successful nanny who is leaving, now might be the time to introduce her. She will be able to say things about the job and your kids that you can't, and she may spot things about the applicants that you would never have noticed. On the other hand, if you have not been entirely happy with your present nanny and if you are parting not entirely on good terms, keep her away at this point.

You will obviously have further questions to ask the nannies at the second interview. You certainly will not have managed to get through the list on pp. 131-3 in one half-hour pre-liminary interview. But the most important thing at this point is to get to know her a bit. You would not, after all, be interviewing her again if she was wildly unsuitable for the job.

The nanny too will certainly have questions, especially as she senses she might actually get the job. Allow her as much time as she needs for these questions. It is far easier to discuss problem areas at this point than it is later, when she is committed to the job. She should expect to meet your previous nanny if you have one. Even if you are not involving her at this stage, you should assure your applicants that they can meet her before they start the job, if they are appointed. If you are not going to let that happen and there is some skeleton in the cupboard about the predecessor, it is probably best to come fairly clean now!

You must contact all the unsuccessful applicants to let them know that they have not got the job. Don't too this too quickly. Don't do it until you are *certain* that at least one of your shortlist will be satisfactory *and* will accept the job. If you are unlucky, your two favoured candidates may turn you down. Then you may want to see again some of those you passed over first time round.

CHOOSING AND STARTING

The final choice can be a nerve-racking experience. It may be, of course, that you will have absolutely no doubt who you want to appoint. But often it is a question of making a difficult decision between two applicants who seem equally good – even if not perfect. At this point:

- Trust your own instincts and those of your kids. Go for the nanny *they* prefer.
- Try picturing the nanny in the job. Say to yourself – am I going to leave the house happily, knowing that the children are in her hands? Will I come back home to someone I will feel comfortable with myself? Will I be able to talk on the same wavelength about the kids? Will I trust her advice? Sometimes posing the question in this direct way helps you come to a decision. I now have no regrets about rejecting a perfectly good nanny who would have been very good with the children – simply because I felt that I myself had nothing in common with her whatsoever. I just couldn't face the idea of coming home to her at the end of the day.

There will normally be some time between making the decision and the nanny starting. Use this time to sort out the details of the contract. Send her a draft of what you have in mind, with the salary you have agreed. If it is a 'full' contract (see pp. 98-100), let her comment and make suggestions about what should be included – particularly with reference to her duties with the children. Our best nanny made it clear at this stage that she would like to be actively involved in choosing toys and other equipment for the kids, so we wrote that into the duties. Finally, make sure you have two copies signed by both parties. She keeps one and you the other (see p. 97).

You (and she) may find a couple more visits useful before she starts the job. This is particularly the case if she has been appointed a long while in advance. *She* will like to keep in touch with you during that intervening period. *You* will want to reassure yourself that she still exists. And the children will feel happier if they start to get to know her before she has charge of them! It is absolutely *essential* to have a few visits if there is to be no overlap period with the old nanny, or if you are not to be at home for a few days at the beginning of the job. The new nanny will need more time to get to know your children's routine, their likes and dislikes, than a quick half-hour on her first morning!

*

Sometimes, when you are having no success with your advert or when the agency is producing no one satisfactory, it can seem that you will never find a good nanny. Don't worry, you will – even if it takes longer than you expected. Your next task is to make the arrangement work – day by day, week by week. That is the subject of the next chapter.

8

Nannies: making it work

The biggest worry about employing a nanny is the fact that you are almost never there to see her at work. She might be wonderful. You might trust her absolutely. But you will still have only the very vaguest notion about what your child does between the time you leave in the morning and the time you come back in the afternoon. The same is true, of course, if you use a childminder or a day nursery. But there you have other parents to share your uncertainties and anxieties with. If you have a nanny (unless you are part of a nanny share – see pp. 155-9), you are on your own.

To make the arrangement a success, you will have to put in a lot of effort yourself. It is not enough to agree with your nanny some laudable, but vague, principle about the children's interests coming first – and then walk out of the front door as if nothing was different in your life. You will have to adjust your own attitudes to fit in with the new arrangement – as well as getting organised in all kinds of practical ways that you might never have thought of. To be certain of success, you will also have to make one big intuitive leap. You will have to start seeing things from your nanny's point of view, as well as your own.

YOUR OWN EXPECTATIONS

Hours

Be realistic. When you employ a nanny, you are not employing someone who will take care of everything the child needs at all hours of the day and night. Do not expect her to work enormously long hours (unless you pay her an appropriately enormous salary!). Most daily nannies work between forty and fifty hours a week. As a regular pattern, that is quite enough – though most nannies will be happy to do a bit extra in evening babysitting or in an emergency. Make sure you *pay* extra, if she works overtime.

It is rather more complicated if you have a live-in nanny. The fact that she is around all the time means that she is (as far as the child is concerned at least) always on duty. And it is not a very pleasant solution for her to shut herself in her room all evening, just to escape the demands. Arrange in advance with her how many evenings you expect her to work (one or two is the norm) and apart from that *try* to deflect the children from her. She will appreciate your effort, even if it doesn't succeed. Remember if you 'just pop out for a few minutes' while she is in the house on an evening off, that is *overtime*. Pay her accordingly.

Very few live-in nannies expect to cope with small babies in the middle of the night. That is normally thought to be the parents' job. If you are breast-feeding, then there is not much point in having the nanny get up anyway. If you are bottle feeding, you could try having a 'one in three rota' – with the job alternating between you, your partner and the nanny. This has the advantage of giving everyone a rest and also having the semblance of 'fairness'. But, if you plan this arrangement, do make it clear to the nanny before she starts.

Stimulation

Don't imagine that your nanny is going to provide hothouse stimulation for your baby all hours of the day. Of course, you want her to do things with him that will entertain him, amuse him and teach him. You want her to sing with him, read books, have dolly tea parties, build castles, go paddling and all the other things (and more) that you might do yourself. But don't come home expecting the nanny to have devoted all day getting him to walk a month in advance of the girl next door, or to have spent three hours drilling him in letters on the fridge door. These kinds of forcing techniques very rarely work and they can do more harm than good, by decidedly putting the child off whatever activity you are trying to encourage. Besides they confuse your own competitiveness with what is really stimulating for *him*.

Any good nanny will know that kids can get an enormous amount out of the everyday chores of life. So expect her to take him to the shops, to have coffee in restaurants with other nannies and children, to the bank and so forth. So long as it doesn't get out of hand (see pp. 149-50), you do actually want him to learn about how you buy things, about how you sometimes have to wait in line and about how you choose what you have in a café. There will still be plenty of time for the more obviously 'educational' activities.

What really matters

Don't expect your nanny to be a carbon copy of you. She will want to do things slightly differently from you. Sometimes it is important to iron these differences out. It is no good, for example, one of you being strict about the child's 'table manners' if the other doesn't care at all. But on many things you will just have to let her do it her way.

Take clothes, for example. You may hate seeing your little girl in pink frills, and want always to dress her in bright red dungarees. Your nanny, on the other hand, may feel much happier if the child looks 'feminine'. Before making this an issue, think whether it really *matters*. It may do. It may be an indication of a lot of other sexist attitudes that you want to protect your child from. And, if that's the case, you will probably have an uphill struggle that won't be over until you change your nanny! But it may be a fairly harmless preference. In this case, swallow your pride and let it be. Remember that your nanny will want to go out with the child and feel that she looks (in her terms) OK. If that means little dresses, it is not going to do you or your daughter much harm.

DAILY ROUTINE

You won't be able to lay down all the details of your nanny's daily routine. The whole point of having a good nanny is that you can trust her to organise your child's day *without* minute-by-minute instructions. But you can offer general principles (on punishment or diet, for example), make specific suggestions (about the local zoo or park) and reassure yourself that you have a procedure for emergencies worked out in advance. You can also have the practical side of life organised so that the nanny finds it easy to do her job well.

Talking

It is very important to find some time most days to talk to your nanny about how things are going and to give her an opportunity to raise any problems. Don't expect her to do this in her own time. If she works from 9.00 to 5.30 and you leave the house the minute she arrives and never return till the dot of 5.30, then you need to increase her hours (and her pay) a little – or get home earlier yourself. Try to overlap with her by 10 minutes or so regularly. Obviously that won't always be possible. But if it never is, you will find you become increasingly out of touch with what your nanny is doing. One day she will hand in her notice and you will not have had the faintest clue that it was coming!

Friends

Your children need a social life and so does your nanny. You cannot expect her to sit in the house day after day, just playing with the kids. If *you* were forced to do that, you would quickly go mad for want of a bit of adult company. So make sure your nanny gets some escape from the house too.

If she has had a job in your area before, or if she was at college there, she will probably already have a network of nanny friends. They will visit each other, plan joint expeditions and may even run their own 'nanny group'. This is the nanny equivalent of a 'mother and toddler club'. They will probably take it in turns to meet in each other's houses. The kids will race around, while the nannies supervise the rumpus and get a chance to have a cup of tea and a chat. Of course, it is not all plain sailing. Nannies do quarrel – and you may discover that the particular group of friends changes. But most good nannies will not let their own personal preferences get in the way too much once your child has established her own firm friendships.

If your nanny is new to the area, you may have to help her get into this sort of network. If any of your friends or colleagues has a nanny, ask them to put her in touch with your nanny. Also look in the paper and newsagents' windows. Some nanny groups advertise. Once she has got one or two contacts, she will quickly find more friends. If you have no other leads, then suggest a 'mother and toddler' club. But be warned. Most nannies feel that they have a lot of common ground with other nannies, not so much with mothers.

You can get to feel that the social life is taking over. More particularly, you may feel a bit concerned that your children are always going out to people you don't know and places you have never been. There are a few things you can do to put your mind at rest:

- Make it quite clear that her nanny friends are welcome in your house. You may feel slightly daunted at the thought of a whole nanny group meeting in your sitting room. But it is a small price to pay for having part of the socialising on *your* territory.
- Try to meet some of these nanny friends. If the nanny group does sometimes meet at your house, drop by one day if you can. But do make it quite clear that you are not 'checking up' on the nanny. And don't be tempted to join in. It is a *nanny* group, not a *mothers'* group.
- Try to find out who the parents of the other nannies' charges are. You may well find that you actually know some of them. I have had several conversations of the 'My goodness, I never realised *you* were Caroline's mother' variety.

- Ask the nanny to leave a note at home of where she has gone, with the phone number if possible. You may want to get in touch with her urgently.
- Suggest that you jointly keep a child's calendar or diary, and that you both write in what you do with the child. That way, the nanny will keep up with what happens at weekends and you will see what is going on during the week.

Remember also that you stand to gain from your nanny being part of a group. Suppose she is ill. If you have some contact with other nannies in her circle, you will probably find that one of them will be prepared to take on your child as an 'extra' for a day – for a reasonable sum. Likewise when your nanny goes on holiday one of her friends may be able to offer the odd day's cover. Always let your nanny help someone else out in this way – if she wants to and if it is not dreadfully inconvenient for you. You may need the same service yourself one day.

Money

If your nanny is going to take your children out, she will need money. You should pay all the expenses of the kids *and* of the nanny – whether they go on a short bus trip to the shops or on a major expedition to the zoo. Don't forget this. Many nannies complain that they end up paying for themselves whenever they go out. Some even claim that they regularly buy food for the children from their own money!

The easiest way of organising this money is to have a family 'jar' or 'purse'. You keep this topped up with money, and the nanny can draw on it whenever she wants for all kinds of day-to-day expenses – food for herself and the kids, transport, nappies and so on. There is no way you can ask her to keep accounts of all this. As in almost everything else, it is important that you *trust* her to spend it appropriately. But don't put too much money in all at once. It is probably a good idea on both sides if you have to discuss any big items of expenditure in advance.

Emergencies

For your own peace of mind, you must discuss with your nanny what will happen in an emergency. Make sure she has your phone number(s) at work, as well as the doctor's number handy. You don't need to tell her exactly what you are doing each day. But you should give her some idea if you are likely to be completely unobtainable. You don't want her to spend hours vainly trying to reach you, when she should be taking the child to the doctor.

If she does not always have a car at work, you will have to think a bit more carefully about your emergency plans. Obviously in a major life-threatening disaster, she could get an ambulance. But she might need instant mobility in less dramatic, but still (from your point of view) pretty urgent, circumstances. Have a list of local taxi numbers pinned up. And see that she has been introduced to some of the immediate neighbours, particularly if there are some who are generally at home during the day.

Bear in mind also that when emergencies happen they can happen to the *nanny*, not the children. Imagine that your nanny is at home with your toddler and three-month-old baby, while you and your partner are both out of reach of the phone all day. She slips and breaks her ankle. Are you confident that she would manage to get herself to the hospital *and* get the kids properly (and happily) taken care of? If you are, then you've got no real worries about your emergency procedures!

PROBLEMS

Everyone has heard horror stories about nannies. Some of these are faintly absurd – the classic 'nanny at the gin bottle' type. Others are frankly nasty. Even the most hardened mother grows a little cold when she hears the one about the apparently normal girl who suddenly went bonkers and took a carving knife to the kids!

How can you prevent disasters? How can you know if things are going wrong?

Foreseeing problems

The first rule is – try to foresee the problems before they arise, so that you don't need to criticise her. It is easy enough, for example, to agree in advance with your nanny that your children *will* not have sweets. That is (or, at least, can seem to be) a joint decision. It is very hard to tell her that she should not *have* given the sweets to the kids. However you dress it up, that is a reprimand. The real difficulty here is that you will quickly become friends with your nanny, as well as being her employer. And friends do not reprimand each other.

This means that you must constantly be predicting the next stage of your child's development and thinking what the areas of difficulty will be. When the baby is still tiny and sleeping most of the day, you should plan what his timetable will be when he is a little older. You should decide, for example, whether you want him regularly *rocked* to sleep, or whether you want him to learn to go to sleep on his own, even at the cost of a bit of crying. That way you will avoid having to tell the nanny to *stop* rocking him after she has been doing it devotedly for several months. A bit later you will have to think about about potty training and whether you are going to be tough or liberal and messy. You will find that it is very awkward (and confusing for the child) to draw your nanny back from a tough approach, once she has started.

You need to make sure that you find time once a month or so for this kind of discussion. Warn the nanny in advance and ask her to give some thought to plans for the future and anything she is beginning to think necessary for the children. Of course, the final decision on all this will be yours. But do involve her. And remember:

- She may have more experience of kids than you have. She will expect that experience to be *respected*, even if not always acted upon.
- It is she who will be putting into practice what you decide. She is on her own with the kids most of the day. She can easily subvert your plans if you don't win her agreement.
- A successful nanny arrangement depends on *consensus*.

Once you have had outright *confrontation* on a few issues, you can be fairly certain that she will not be staying with you much longer.

- The only time that you can successfully *tell* her what to do is at the very beginning of her employment. If you have particularly strong views on any aspect of childcare, you must make them clear then.

How to recognise that things are going wrong

The clearest sign that all is not well is your own anxiety. Suppose you find youself looking in the kitchen bin to see whether the kids had junk food *again* for lunch. Suppose you find yourself ringing up to see if the nanny really is in all day like she said she would be. If you are doing this kind of checking, you can be fairly certain that something is amiss. Of course, you may be *over*anxious. You may be expecting too much of the wrong kind of thing (see pp. 142-3). Try explaining what is bothering you to a friend, preferably one with kids and a nanny. If she thinks that you are not being unreasonable, then you really have got problems. There are too many potential problems to list. But the following are some particularly common ones.

The nanny's social life can begin to take over. Just occasionally the round of tea parties and coffee mornings gets out of hand. It is not that there are too many social occasions, but rather that they are arranged entirely for the *nanny's* convenience, not the child's. You can even find that a group of nannies are making joint expeditions to the local sun-beds – leaving one to look after the kids outside, while the others perfect their tans! Of course, the dividing line between this and *useful* socialising can be hard to draw. Find out as accurately as possible what is going on and ask yourself directly – is that doing my child any good at all? is it reasonable for the nanny to be doing that in the time that I pay for?

Some nannies are what I call 'buggy-pushers'. That is, they spend most of the day wandering round the town, window-shopping and visiting friends who work in boutiques.

This doesn't matter *too* much when the child is tiny. In fact it gives the nanny of a very little baby something to do! But for an energetic toddler five hours a day strapped in the buggy is sheer cruelty. She will usually give up and go to sleep – lulled by the rocking and the boredom. Again try to find out as accurately as possible what is going on. But you could also try the 'sleep test'. Is the kid regularly up and lively at 11 o'clock in the evening on the days she is cared for by the nanny, but in bed and asleep by 7 under your charge? In that case *suspect* that she is not getting enough exercise and stimulus. (Don't misuse this test. It is gross *disparity* in sleeping habits that you are looking for. Don't blame the nanny just because you've got a poor sleeper!)

Some nannies fail to adapt as the child grows older. They may be very skilled at looking after a small baby, but not cope well with a demanding and determined toddler. It is not that caring for a tiny infant is *easy*. Far from it. Many of us are driven to distraction by the mess and the screaming. But babies do give the nanny quite a lot of free time – for watching television, writing letters or whatever. And they don't impose their will in the clever way that a two-year-old can. Nor do they demand literally hours of help with their Sticklebricks or Duplo! Watch out that your nanny makes the adjustment. Some don't. They will have little idea about *outwitting* the kid in the way that *every* toddler-carer must. And they will positively refuse to put Sticklebricks before the afternoon soap. Observe what is going on quite carefully if you get a chance. Try the 'sleep test' again. And remember it *is* hard work looking after a toddler – but that is what you are paying her to do.

What to do about it

Do not be optimistic about solving any of these problems unless you really catch them in the bud. You can *try* keeping a closer check on what the nanny does each day, perhaps getting her to complete a diary. But unless you started this in the very beginning, it will look like rather aggressive 'policing'. You can *try* making specific suggestions about activities. But if there's an underlying problem, this will probably have only a marginal effect. She might rather grudgingly get the paints out a bit more often, but there won't be a real change of attitude.

You do not actually know what happens for most of the time you are away. You cannot grill your children on the subject. It is not fair on them to make them into your spies – and if they are under three they are not going to be reliable informants anyway. You have to trust your nanny as she is, not imagine that you can 'reform' her. Be realistic. If she is not working as you want and you start to put pressure on her, she will sooner or later (probably sooner) leave. That is probably for the best.

If the worst happens

If you discover that the nanny has done something really heinous, sack her. Don't give her a second chance – even if it leaves you completely in the lurch. But remember:

- Do be certain of your facts, especially if she is an old and trusted nanny. Don't rely on vague hearsay.
- Even if it goes against the grain, pay her salary in advance in lieu of notice. The last thing you want at this point is to get involved in an argument about money.
- Take a moment to ask yourself if it really was so serious. Intentional violence against your kids is one thing. But accidents (even serious ones) *can* happen when they are being looked after by the most loving and responsible people.

If you do end up suddenly without a nanny (for this or any other reason), you will need emergency childcare tomorrow. You may be lucky and have friends who can help you out. Or you or your partner may be able to take a few days off work. But if not, get in touch with an agency supplying qualified *nurses*. These agencies are fearfully expensive, but they are used to providing qualified medical staff at a moment's notice. They will get you someone who, even if not a nanny, can certainly be relied upon. This will give you the few days you need to find a temporary nanny through a more regular employment agency.

THE NANNY'S POINT OF VIEW

Being a nanny is not really a job for life. There are no career or promotion prospects – except in a few day nurseries. There are some jobs in infant schools or hospitals. But in these the nanny (or nursery nurse) is always subordinate to teachers and trained general nurses. The pay too is dreadfully low. It may seem a lot to you, when you pay her out of your own wages. It may also be quite sufficient for a girl still living with her parents. But just start calculating what kind of mortgage you could get on the salary you pay her. Would it be enough for even one quarter of a small flat in your area? As soon as you do these sums, you will see that there is a limit to how long anyone can go on being a nanny – that is, if they want any independence.

For all these reasons a job as a nanny is only a staging post for most girls, even those who are trained. For some it is a staging post on the way to marriage and having children (and maybe becoming a childminder (see pp. 163-4) when her children are a bit older). For others it is a staging post to a different kind of career after further training – either in teaching or one of the 'caring professions'. You will find that many nannies have entered their training course fully intending to move on after a few years. Others realise the limitations of the job only after they have been in it for a while.

Temporary or not, there are a lot of simple things that *you* can do to make your nanny's job more enjoyable. This is not just altruism of course. The happier she is the better nanny she will be.

Most nannies dislike

- An employer who is often late. Everyone accepts that you will occasionally not make it home when you said. But it is infuriating for a nanny *regularly* to be trapped holding the baby, twenty minutes after you said you would be back.

- A house that is dirty and untidy. Remember it is your nanny's working environment. *You* may not mind your dirty underwear everywhere. But she very well might – and it is not her job to clear it up.
- An employer who goes back on agreed rules for the children. You are making your nanny's life impossible if you don't follow at weekends the rules you have agreed for her during the week. It may be hard enough for her anyway to restrict their sweets to 'one a day'. But if you have given them a whole *packet* of toffees at the weekend, she has no chance!
- Working in a house with really dilapidated baby equipment. Again, *you* might not mind the buggy with the broken foot rest or the dodgy wheel. You might even feel quite to attached to it! But buggies and all the rest are the tools of the nanny's trade. She will expect them to be, not necessarily new, but at least presentable. The same goes for kids' clothes. It is an insult to her professionalism if there is nothing decent to dress them in.
- Being treated as a general dogsbody. Most nannies are happy to do their bit in an emergency – to wait in, for example, until the man has come to repair the washing machine. But don't constantly ask her to run errands for you. And don't arrange for her to look after someone else's children as well – even for an hour – without consulting her first.
- An employer who never says 'thank you'. You would never imagine that this could apply to you. But you would be amazed how many nannies complain that the mother has never expressed any gratitude for what they do. Even more say that their employer has never given them a present – not even at Christmas or birthday time. You *must* be grateful for what she does. *Show* her that you are.

You can't be a *perfect* employer. You are probably overworked, and you are bound to have days when you feel cross and irritable. But you will succeed better than most if you ask yourself from time to time – 'How is this job working out for the nanny?'

Finally, remember that when nannies get together the first thing they talk about is how much they are paid. They admit this themselves. The employer's 'generosity' is constantly under scrutiny. What can you do about this? Obviously you should make sure that you are paying the going rate for the job. You should not risk losing a good nanny for the sake of a couple of pounds a week. But you should also gently remind the nanny from time to time of her 'conditions of service' and her working hours. When they are in a group nannies do tend to compare cash with cash and to forget that some of them work much longer hours and have different duties. They don't alway see that £100 per week can be wildly generous for some jobs and ridiculously mean for others.

WHEN SHE LEAVES

In the end, she is bound to leave. If you are parting on good terms, it will be sad but not difficult.

- Make sure that she meets the new nanny. She will probably have grown very attached to your kids and will want to have some contact with the person who is going to take over. It is also very much to *your* advantage if she explains the nature of the job to her replacement, from a nanny's point of view.
- Explain to her if you are slightly changing the duties of the new nanny (adding cleaning, for example), or if you are paying the replacement at a different rate. Explain to her why. They will only talk about it as soon as they meet. Better to come clean now than worry about them comparing notes.
- Mark her leaving in some way – with a little party and presents. Don't go over the top with a great emotional occasion. But some kind of 'special event' will help the kids take in the fact that she is leaving and won't be back on Monday morning as usual.
- Encourage her to come and visit the children. Invite her for

celebrations at Christmas and birthday time. Don't fall into the trap of thinking it better to have a sharp break, because meetings will only upset the kids. They may well upset them a bit. But for very young children a dearly loved nanny who has just disappeared might as well be dead. Don't subject them to that kind of bereavement unnecessarily.

Things will be much more difficult if the old nanny has been sacked, has left suddenly or resigned over some major disagreement:

- If relations haven't entirely broken down, try to get her to meet the new nanny. But don't arrange things so that they have a long time on their own together!
- Do still encourage her to keep in contact with the kids. You and she might have fallen out. But the children may well still be fond of her, and she of them. Even if she seems reluctant to visit, keep up sending Christmas and birthday cards if you can and the odd photo of the kids. That way, she doesn't entirely disappear from their lives.

NANNY SHARING

Sharing a nanny with another family may seem the ideal way of having all the advantages of a nanny at considerably less cost. This kind of arrangement can work marvellously. You each pay rather less than you would for your own nanny. The nanny ends up getting a considerably fatter salary. And your child has the benefit of the company of the other child or children. But it is not all plain sailing. Dealing with another family as well as with the nanny brings its own problems. There are disadvantages as well as advantages over the standard nanny arrangement.

Finding a sharer

Most shares are arranged by word of mouth. You may know a friend (or the friend of a friend) who is looking for childcare at about the same time as you are. But there are ways of finding a 'sharer' even if you do not know one personally. Local branches of the NCT sometimes run a register of those looking for a share, as do branches of the Working Mothers Association. Some agencies (particularly local ones) will also try and join you up with another family. You can even try advertising for a partner in the local paper or *The Lady* – and then advertising together for a shared nanny.

Whatever way you find someone to join with you, think carefully about these points before you commit yourself irrevocably:

- Are your needs compatible? Nanny shares work best if each party has roughly the same regular working hours. You will strike disaster if one of you works a five day week, nine to five, and the other must often work late or start early.
- Where does your sharer live? It is crazy to contemplate a share with someone miles away or in the 'wrong direction' between your home and your work. One of the children has to be transported each day. Don't commit yourself to unmanageable travelling.
- Is your general approach to childcare roughly the same as your sharer's? The nanny won't be able to apply one set of rules to one child, one to another. So make sure that you agree on things like food, punishment, swearing or whatever.
- What are the ages of the children concerned? There is no *right* answer here. But you need to be aware of the consequences of different age gaps. You will be giving the nanny a very tough job if you put two (or more) babies in her care. Obviously it *is* manageable. Those who care for twins manage, after all. But she will deserve a very good salary for her efforts. On the other hand, if one child is considerably older than the other, they are likely to get little (social) benefit from being with one another. And the nanny's attention might be monopolised by a demanding three-year-old, at the expense of a placid seven-month-old.

What to discuss in advance

Apart from the details of tax and National Insurance (see pp. 88-9), you must discuss some of the important practical arrangements before you even advertise for a nanny. Though final decisions on some of these should wait until you have had a chance to talk to the nanny herself.

In whose house are the children going to be based? If the children are based at your sharer's house, you will have the inconvenience of having to get them up, dressed and round to the nanny (like to the childminder) before you go off to work yourself. On the other hand, if they are at your place, you will come to feel that it has rather been 'taken over' by kids during the hours you are not there. And the signs of them (and the damage) will still be evident, even after they have gone home.

Most shares tend to alternate between one house and the other. This is certainly the fairest system (in expense, as well as convenience), but it is more emotionally disruptive. You will find yourself in the middle of the night trying to remember whether or not it is *your* house on Monday...! And the nanny may much prefer one place to the other – either because it is more convenient for transport, or because it is bigger for the kids.

What equipment will you need to duplicate or to buy specially? This is one of the biggest expenses of nanny sharing. If you are asking the nanny to look after two babies or toddlers, you will certainly need to buy a double buggy. And if you are basing her at both houses, then you will have to buy *two* double buggies – unless you can conveniently manage to transport just the one from one house to the other, day after day. Likewise you will need two cots at each place if the kids are still having a nap in the day – maybe at the same time. And, of course, two car seats in any car she is going to drive. All this is going to take up space in your house, as well as cost money.

What is going to happen if one of the kids is ill? Will everyone move to his house then, whatever the normal arrangements? And what about holidays? Will you, your sharer and the nanny all agree to take your holidays at the same time?

You must also be realistic about the end of the arrangement. Between you and your sharer, you must decide what is going to happen if one of you decides to withdraw from the arrangement for any reason. How will the expenses of the extra equipment be divided at that point? Will the remaining party guarantee to keep the nanny on, perhaps at a reduced total salary? Will you attempt to find a new sharer? And what will happen if you can't? If one of the families has a new baby, will the arrangement still continue?

When you have decided all this (at least in principle), tell the nanny – or even write it into her contract. It affects her job. She is bound to be worried if no plans have been made for the arrangement falling through.

Disadvantages

The *advantages* of a nanny share are obvious – lower cost for you, higher pay for the nanny, company for the kids. But before you optimistically launch into a share, go over the *dis*advantages in your mind.

- The nanny will not be able to give you the *service* that your own individual nanny can. If she is looking after two small kids, who travel round in a double buggy, she will find it pretty hard to get to the health clinic or doctor's for immunisations and the like. Trundling round the shops looking for right fitting shoes for one of them will be next to impossible. You will have to do all this at weekends.
- You will always lack flexibility with a nanny share. You won't, for example, be able to ask the nanny to come away with you for a few days, because she is committed to looking after your share-partner's kids.
- You will not have the advantage of just being able to walk out of the door in the morning, leaving the nanny to the kids – whether they are dressed and breakfasted or not. Or if you do have that advantage, you will have the accompanying disadvantage of someone else's kids racing

round your house. You will find that you are even less tolerant of the damage done by your sharer's children than you are of that done by your own!

- You will have two lots of people to make arrangements and decisions with – not just the nanny, but the other family as well. You may find that it is almost unbelievably complicated to arrange all to take your holidays at the same time. And even things like potty training or 'table manners' may require a tripartite conference!
- It is very easy to meet a circumstance in which your interests clash with those of the other family. Suppose your child needs a periods of special attention for some reason – perhaps because she has been ill, or maybe just because she still needs a lot of help with a new trike she had for Christmas. How will this fit in with the needs of your sharer's child?

In some ways a nanny share has many of the drawbacks of a childminder or day nursery, with few of their advantages. You can't, for example, easily extricate yourself from the arrangement. You can't be certain (as you can be with a nursery) that your carer won't be ill. Before you decide on a nanny share, think whether you wouldn't be better served by one of these other options – which the two final chapters consider.

9

Childminders and childminding

A childminder looks after other people's children in her own home. Childminding has had a bad press. Mention 'minding' and some people immediately conjure up a vision of rows of pathetic toddlers strapped into their buggies and left for hours on end in front of the television – the minder nowhere to be seen. Child*minding* can be almost a by-word for ignorant, unstimulating 'care'.

Don't let that image put you off. There certainly are some dreadful childminders, like there are dreadful nannies. But many provide a good standard of care and some are truly excellent. They may be trained NNEBs or qualified nurses or primary school teachers, who for whatever reason prefer to work from home. In fact, if you are looking for a *mature* carer (say in her thirties or forties) with some relevant training, and if you like the idea of a home environment rather than a nursery, it is probably best to consider a childminder first. Most good nannies will have left the private nanny market (either for marriage and childminding or to take further qualifications) by the time they are 25.

Childminders are also relatively cheap, probably the cheapest form of full-time care, unless you miraculously qualify for a free day nursery. Though where you live will make a difference here. A good 'professional' childminder in London will cost as much as a newly trained daily nanny in the North.

REGISTERED CHILDMINDERS

By law, anyone who looks after children in her own home, 'for reward', for more than two hours a day must be registered with the local Social Services Department. Registration is only unnecessary if the child is a close relative of the minder (perhaps a grandchild). Otherwise anyone who minds a child without registration is acting illegally and could, in the end, be fined. *Never* use an unregistered childminder. If you find someone you would like to mind your child but who is not registered, get her to register first.

What registration involves

Registration is meant to ensure that a childminder is a 'fit person' to look after children and that the physical conditions of her home are satisfactory for their care. Different Social Services Departments interpret this in different ways.

Some make quite extensive inquiries about a potential childminder, taking up references from health visitors, Housing Departments or even from the police. And some require that potential minders attend a short course. That requirement may not mean very much in itself. There is not very much you can learn about childcare in a day, if you didn't know it already. But it probably discourages some of the least suitable from seeking registration. And it will also introduce the new childminder to a local group of keen and experienced minders.

Other Departments are much more limited in the checks they carry out. The minimum you can assume of a childminder who has been registered is that at the time of registration:

- neither she nor her partner had a record of offences against children, and that they had not had any children taken into care
- she was reasonably healthy (often a chest X-ray will have been required)
- her home was a safe environment for young children (with checks on fire precautions, on the heating of the house, toilet facilities, etc.)

Registration does not mean that the childminder is good

and conscientious, or even competent. It simply means that there was no obvious reason why she should be refused permission to mind. You should always check out everything again yourself – and don't assume that you can take *anything* for granted simply because the woman is registered. After all, the house might have been safe when the Social Services Department visited. But who is to check that the fire guard is *always* in place? The Department is supposed to keep in regular touch with registered childminders, partly to ensure that the conditions of minding remain satisfactory. This can be a really valuable support to childminders when it does happen. But it doesn't always. Some registered minders claim they have had no contact with their Social Services Department for over two years.

What registration allows

A minder will be registered to take care of a maximum number of children (including her own), and there will normally be some restriction on their ages. A common arrangement is to allow three children under five – with no more than one being under a year, and no more than two between one and two. The minder's own school-aged children don't usually count. But there may be a special arrangement for her to mind other people's children after school and in the holidays.

The only *direct* benefit that follows registration is free milk. Every registered minder can claim one third of a pint of milk per day for each child she is minding. The *indirect* benefits of registration are probably more important. Registration will put the minder in touch with local groups of childminders who often give each other advice and practical help, or organise playgroups and outings. Some Social Services Departments may even lend safety equipment and expensive toys to newly registered minders.

VARIETIES OF CHILDMINDERS

Women start childminding for a wide variety of different reasons, both good and bad. Some drift into it as a way of earning a bit of money while they are at home with their own kids. Others see it as a profession. It won't ever make them rich, but they are committed to it as a skill and a service.

It will help *you* make your choice of a childminder if you reflect a little on the different backgrounds and motivations that bring women into childminding. This is not to say that the 'professional' minder is always better than the 'drifter'. There are excellent and disastrous minders in all categories. But if you are starting from scratch looking for a childminder, you need to know that some categories are safer than others.

The professional childminder

The professional minder works on a long-term basis. Any kind of trivial reason could have encouraged her to start minding. It might have been a spur of the moment decision when she was looking after her own children at home. But now she sees it as her full-time, permanent job.

Her background is sometimes in education or childcare – maybe a nanny, teacher or nurse. For many of these women it may well seem more attractive to work from home as their own boss, than to return to outside work at perhaps a fairly junior level after a few years off bringing up the kids. Other professional minders have no particular training in childcare. They may have been secretaries, shop assistants or solicitors. But they found they got positive enjoyment from looking after children – and that they had a positive talent for it. Childminding, which demands no formal qualifications, can give them an instant career in what they are good at.

A professional minder will tend to be more imaginative and enterprising in her day-to-day care of the children in her charge. She will also be more involved in the organisation of childminding in a wider sense. She will probably be active in the National Childminding Association (NCMA – a group that coordinates minders throughout the country and provides them with information and support) and have links with the local Social Services Department, local minders' groups, playgroups, toy libraries and so forth. Some even manage to get grants from charities or the Local Authority to take their children on outings to the zoo or the seaside.

A few professional minders do 'double-handed' minding. That is, with the agreement of the Social Services Department, they take on a helper and become registered for up to six children. With a trained nanny or primary teacher, this can turn what is officially 'childminding' to what is in effect a mini-nursery class in a home. For many mothers this may seem the ideal system of childcare – combining the directed stimulus of a nursery class with the informality of small numbers and a private house.

Casual minders

The main difference between a casual minder and a professional is that the casual minder does not intend to carry on childminding in the long term. She has her own children at home and opts for childminding to earn a bit of money before she can return to outside work, when the kids go to school. There is, of course, nothing morally wrong about this – and it may make good financial sense for the childminder. But it does mean that the minder is likely to be less engaged in the whole activity, less inclined to invest time and energy into obtaining play equipment or keeping up to date with new developments in childcare, more likely to want to 'fit the children in' around household chores, shopping and visits to her friends.

Remember motherhood on its own isn't a sufficient qualification for being a good childminder. People often assume that any mother, just because of her experience with her own kids, will act in a responsible and caring way to the children she minds. This simply isn't so. Some mothers are lousy mothers. And besides, looking after someone else's child is quite a different experience from looking after your own. It requires a different range of talents. Professional childminders realise this. Casual minders may not.

Friends

Sometimes one of your friends who is based at home with her own kids may volunteer to register as a childminder just so that she can look after your baby. There is no formal obstacle to this. Most Social Services Departments understand these arrangements – and are in fact grateful that your friend takes the trouble to register properly. From your point of view the advantages are obvious. You are leaving your child with someone you already know and trust, and whose views on childcare are (presumably) close to your own.

Some of these arrangements work exceedingly well. But others simply disrupt your friendship. It is not easy to turn a friend into a childminder. You are likely to feel awkward negotiating with her about money. It will be even more difficult complaining about any aspect of her care. Don't imagine that, because she has looked after your child very successfully on a Saturday afternoon, there will be no problems when she is doing it full-time. However much you agree in general terms about the 'philosophy' of childcare, she is bound to do some things differently from how you'd like. And she is bound to treat your child differently from the way she treats her own. If you don't think you could raise these issues openly without losing your friendship, you shouldn't even consider this type of arrangement.

To sum up

There are no hard and fast rules about choosing a childminder, no hard and fast divisions between the different types of minder. The description above of the professional minder is a bit too rosy. No childminder is quite that perfect. And, of course, the fact that she is a trained teacher or is intending to continue in childminding for the foreseeable future is no *guarantee* that she will be any good at it. There are some primary school teachers that I wouldn't let within a mile of my children! On the other hand, some people who take up minding in a quite casual way turn out to be absolutely excellent. Even if they only intend to be minding for a few years, they may still put a great deal into it for that short period. And some minders who start out doing it casually or 'just for a friend' find that it suits them so well that they end up as 'professionals'.

Don't go searching for the perfect professional minder. She might never exist. But it will help you to find and judge a *good* minder, if you have some notion of what the ideal professional might be like.

HOW TO FIND A CHILDMINDER

When to start

If you want to find a childminding place for a baby, *start early* – as soon as he is born, if you intend to return to work within a few months. In some areas good childminders are in short supply. And there is particular pressure on baby places, since most minders are only registered to take one child under one year old. Find a good minder as soon as you can. Be prepared to pay her a retainer (see pp. 173-4) for a couple of months, to secure the place.

Contacts

To find a good childminder, you need to get access to the 'minder network'. There are two main ways of doing this:

- Personal contact. Ask anyone you know who has used a minder for a recommendation. Ask your midwife, your health visitor and your GP. Follow up anyone they suggest, if they sound roughly like what you want. Don't bother too much at this stage about details of where they live and so forth. What you need is contact with a good minder. She may not have a vacancy. She may quite clearly be in an inconvenient part of town for you. But the chances are that she will be able to put you in touch with someone who would suit you.
- Ring up your local Social Services Department and ask to speak to the childminding adviser or the under 5's adviser. Tell them that you are looking for a childminder. They will then either send you a complete list of registered childminders in the area where you live and the area of your work. This will normally include the name of a

childminder-coordinator for the area, who keeps track of the vacancies currently open. Or they will just give you the names of minders with vacancies in those areas. Try, if you can, to get the complete list, especially if you are looking for a place some months ahead. The Social Services Department may not always know about *predicted* vacancies some months ahead. Try also to get as many names in as many places as possible. Occasionally the Department will try to *tell* you where your childminder should be. Don't let them. Obviously you will want to consider minders very close to your home or to your work first. But there may also be good minders on your route between home and work – or near where your partner works.

Maybe you have no personal contacts. Perhaps the Social Services Department turns out to be unhelpful, or manages to produce no suitable minder – particularly a problem in rural areas, where minders are much thinner on the ground. You could try getting in touch with the NCMA, who aim to provide help and information for women seeking minders, as well as for minders themselves. But if you still draw a blank, then you may have to consider advertising. It is worth a short ad in the local paper or the local newsagent, asking either for a registered childminder *or* a woman who is not already registered, but is prepared to go through the registration procedure. Don't waste words. But don't forget to put the hours you will require each week. That's what is crucial for most childminders to know.

> Childminder wanted. Chesterton or New Hospital area. 8.30 to 5.30 Monday to Friday. Must be registered, or willing to register. Tel. Cambridge 366666 (6-8pm).

An advert like this may pick up a registered childminder that you have otherwise missed. It may also attract someone who had perhaps been considering becoming a childminder, but needed an bit of incentive. The registration process may take several months, but the Social Services Department will usually turn a blind eye if you start using the woman immediately – as long as they know about it and know that the registration is going through. But remember you are bound to be taking a greater risk if you engage someone who has never minded before, doesn't have the full range of equipment an experienced minder would have and doesn't really understand quite what is involved.

The first visit

When you have got the name of someone with a vacancy who sounds as if she might be suitable, ring her up and arrange to go and visit. (If she's not on the phone, forget it. You are going to need to get in touch with your childminder at short notice.) The best procedure is similar to that recommended for finding a nanny (see pp. 128-38). You need a preliminary session to find out if there's any chance that you suit each other. Then, if the first session goes all right, you will want a second meeting to talk about things in more detail. But remember that the 'balance of power' is rather different with a childminder. You are not simply interviewing her to decide whether or not you will employ her. She is offering a professional service – and she is (at least in part) interviewing you to decide whether *she* is prepared to take *you* on. You are not in control in the same way.

Choose a time for your first visit during her working hours, when her other minded children are around. That way you will be able to observe how she relates to those in her charge. In general, use the first meeting to check out on those things that are most important to you. Obviously these will differ from person to person. The list that follows will give you some idea of the things you might be looking for, things you will want to find out:

- How long has she been childminding? How long does she intend to go on doing it? This will not only give you some idea of how 'professional' she is. But there's a practical side too. She may only intend to go on minding until her four-year-old is settled in school. If you are looking for a long-term place for your baby, this obviously won't do.

- How long have most of her children stayed with her? Where have they gone on to? Beware if she seems to have had a very quick turnover – particularly if the kids have gone on to other childminders. Quite a lot of mothers use a childminder while they are waiting for a nursery place, and so may only be with her for a short time. Very few people change from childminder to childminder unless the first has been in some way unsatisfactory.

- How many children does she look after? The permitted numbers for a registered childminder are calculated as if they were *full-time* places. That is, a childminder registered for three kids might actually make that up with twelve part-timers. That is fine if you are looking for a part-time place. But it is not so good if you are wanting a full-time place for your child. There will be constant comings and goings, different children every day, and the pace of life will be set by those there for just a few hours. If you want a full-time place, try to find a childminder who has other full-time kids – or at least only a limited number of part-timers.

- Try to find out about the daily routine. Does she find time to read to the children? And to play and talk with them? How long would a toddler normally spend in a playpen each day? How much television do the kids usually watch? How much time do they spend trundling around the neighbourhood? Some childminders take their minded kids to deliver their own children to different schools in the morning, pick them up at lunch-time, take them back after lunch and pick them up again at the end of the day. That can be a regular two-and-a-half hours of each day spent in the buggy, before she has even started on the shopping, the post office and all the rest!

- What are her views on potty training? On discipline? On 'table manners'? On any other aspect of childcare that is important to you? Remember, you will be able to *instruct* a childminder even less easily than you could a nanny. So it is even more important to make sure that you see eye to eye on most of these points.

- What kind of special outings do the children go on? Do they visit play-groups or 'one-o-clock clubs' (playgroups organised with childminders especially in mind)? Do they travel in the minder's car to these groups? If so, what kind of child restraints does she have fitted?

- Is the minder a member of the NCMA? Does she have links with other minders in the neighbourhood? This can be a great help, if your minder is ill. Minders in a group will often act as emergency cover for their friends – which will prevent you having to take extra days off work or desperately ring around the non-working mothers in the area. But remember that this is for *emergency* cover. You don't want your kids being regularly dumped elsewhere, so that your minder can go to the dry cleaners, the hairdressers or whatever.

- Does she have good relations with local Health Visitors? It is often helpful if the Health Visitor can see your child while she is at the childminder's – or if the minder can take a baby to the clinic for his regular checks.

- Does she provide food for toddlers? All minders will expect *you* to supply milk for babies – make sure she has a freezer, if you are intending to give her breast milk (see pp. 47-8). Some will provide lunch for the older children, either for extra cost or included in the daily fee. If she does do this, what kind of food is it? If you feel very strongly about junk food, bring that issue out straight away. Some of the best minders provide weekly menus for their mothers. Ask to see one.

- Are the house and garden safe? Look out for the danger areas – the fire or other heating system, the stairs, the kitchen appliances, the garden gate, the pond. If *you* were looking after three toddlers in this house, would *you* feel confident that they wouldn't come to (unnecessary) harm? And is she properly insured in case any child is injured in an accident in her home? (The NCMA offers a special insurance policy to minders, which also covers them against the damage your kids might do to other people's property, while in the minder's care!)

- Is the house a place where you would *like* your child to spend most of her waking hours? Are there plenty of toys of different types – toys for being messy, for fantasy games, for banging and clashing, toys for building and fitting together, books and paints? Has the minder made an effort to make the minded children feel 'at home' in her house? Are their pictures up on the walls? Do they have their own box or drawer where they can keep their special things?
- Find out, if you can, if she has an 'emergency routine' worked out. If she had to take one of her kids urgently to the hospital, how would she get there quickly? How would she cope with the other children?
- What other adults are likely to be around the house during the day? It is no use reassuring yourself that the minder doesn't smoke, if her eldest daughter is at home smoking forty a day!

Remember, it is not a good idea to go in and 'interview' the minder, as you might a potential nanny. The minder will be wanting to find out as much about you, as you about her. Try to raise most of the issues in the course of general conversation. And keep the direct questions ('May I ask you if you smoke?') to a minimum. Most important of all, *use your eyes*. Particularly take note of how the other kids behave. How does she relate to them? Do they approach her often – for help, reassurance, comfort? Even if the minder can put on an act of total devotion to her charges, no toddler will be induced to feign affection for someone who neglects her most of the day.

You may think that the childminder you have seen is a possible one for you. But you may also feel that you would like to meet some other minders before you commit yourself. Explain to the childminder you have visited that you would like some time to think and that you have arranged to see some other minders. Don't try to conceal the fact that you are going to see others. Childminders have their mafia! The chances are that she will find out that you have been doing the rounds. And don't imagine that you have a lot of time. Few childminders will hold open a vacancy just because you have said you *might* be interested. Get round to see the other childminders quickly.

The second visit

When you have narrowed down your choice to perhaps one or two childminders, you will want to go back for another visit. This is your opportunity to raise anything you didn't bring up the first time – and also to discuss details of money and the exact hours of care that you will be needing.

- Ask the childminder what her hourly charge will be. Many minders operate a sliding scale, charging their poorest clients somewhat less than the better off. Don't be tempted to abuse this system. No minder is going to be taken in if you try to pass yourself off as a pauper. And she will probably spread the word about you around the other minders. Remember also that she may be paying tax and National Insurance out of what you give her. She counts as self-employed – which is simpler for you. Unlike with a nanny, you will not have to have any dealings with the Inland Revenue yourself. But, just because *you* are not working out the deductions each week, don't imagine that she is 'taking home' all you pay her.
- Make sure you know what the charge includes. Will you, for example, pay extra for any playgroup fees? What will you be expected to provide for your child – nappies? babywipes and changing equipment? a packed lunch?
- How much will you pay if your child is absent for any period? Will there be any charge if the minder is ill?
- At what intervals will the fees be renegotiated?
- Explain as carefully as you can the hours of care that you will need. Don't underestimate your needs. It is a recipe for disaster to claim at this stage that you will collect your child at 5.30, if you *know* that half the week you won't actually make it until 5.45. Think also if you are ever likely to need a more flexible arrangement – perhaps because you sometimes have to work overtime in the evening or start

early. You can't assume that your childminder will be happy to take your child from 7 am, just because she is at home. She has her own family and her rest to think about. So raise the problem at the very beginning. And offer to pay extra for 'anti-social hours', if that seems appropriate. Remember too that if you choose just four-and-a-half days to start with, you won't necessarily be able to increase this to five days when you want. The childminder may have filled the remaining half day with a part-time child. Her registration won't then *allow* her to increase your hours.

- Ask her at this stage if she has plans for any holiday. You may be able to tie in your holiday with hers. If you can't do that, does she have any back-up arrangements?

Once you have been through this series of questions, you should be able to make your mind up fairly quickly. Don't rush, of course. But don't delay needlessly – or you may lose the place.

THE FORMALITIES

Preliminary agreement and retainer

If you are booking a place for some time ahead, the childminder will probably require a weekly cash 'retainer' in order to keep the place open for you. If she is well organised, she will ask you to sign a preliminary contract (see the example on p. 174) – including an agreement to pay perhaps half the weekly fee until the child actually starts.

A document of this kind doesn't give you or the childminder any practical legal protection. In any case it wouldn't be worth anyone's while to go to law. But (as with a contract with a nanny) it is helpful to both sides to have the agreement laid out in writing. It minimises the risk of misunderstanding about who is paying what and when.

Agreement to childmind

It has been agreed that Isobel Bradley shall childmind Rachel Lucy Carlisle (age 6 months) at 7 Alpha Crescent, Hereford from 2.2.89. The following days and times have been reserved:Monday to Friday, 8.30 am to 6.00 pm.

A retainer of £30 per week has been agreed in order to hold open the above vacancy. This retainer is to be paid from 6.10.88 until 2.2.89, on which date the childminding is due to start. Payment should be made weekly, in advance. Two weeks' notice is required for termination of this agreement.

Isobel Bradley (childminder) 7 Alpha Crescent, Hereford.

Sarah Carlisle (parent), 16 Searle Avenue, Hereford.
5.10.88.

Contract and information sheet

All good childminders will provide a written contract (see the example opposite). This will include details of the financial agreement, the weekly hours and any particular arrangements for food, outings and supplies. In addition she should ask you to fill in an 'information sheet', giving emergency contact numbers and any important information about the child.

The information sheet should cover the following topics:

- Home phone number and daytime contact address and phone number for both father and mother. An additional contact number (close relative or friend) in case both parents are unavailable.

Agreement to childmind

between

Isobel Bradley (childminder),
7 Alpha Crescent,
Hereford

and
Sarah and Jon Carlisle
(parents),
16 Searle Avenue,
Hereford

Name of child: Rachel Lucy Carlisle (born 20.4.88).

Times of minding: 8.30 am – 6.00 pm, Monday to Friday. Extra hours may be arranged in the morning (from 7.00 am) by prior agreement. No minding can be arranged after 6.00 pm or at weekends.

Start of contract: 2.1.89.

Payment: The regularly hourly charge is £2. This is payable weekly, in advance, on a Monday. Any hour before 8.30 am will be charged at the rate of £3 per hour. Half rates are payable if the child is absent through illness or if the absence is notified one week in advance. Otherwise full rates are payable. No charge is made if the childminder is ill or unable to take the child for any other reason. The charges will be revised annually on 1 January.

Payment for extras: The parents will pay fees for a twice weekly playgroup (currently £1.50 per morning). Any other payments (entrance fees, fares for excursions) to be agreed in advance.

Food etc: The parents will provide baby-milk, all baby-food, nappies and all nappychanging equipment (baby-wipes etc.) The childminder will provide 'family meals', drinks, juice etc.

Holidays: The dates of the childminder's holiday 1989 are 2 – 13 August. This is in addition to all public holidays.

The parents give their consent for the childminder to take the child on outings both on foot, by public transport and in her car. The child will always be properly restrained when travelling in the car. The parents also consent to the childminder obtaining immediate medical treatment for the child if it seems to her necessary.

Signed: Isobel Bradley
Sarah and Jon Carlisle　　　　　*Date*: 11.12.88.

- Name, address and phone number of child's doctor and health visitor. Address of the clinic attended.
- Names of any other person who may collect the child.
- Details of the child's immunisations and a general health record.

In addition it can be useful to make a note of:

- Normal daily routine, especially for a baby or young toddler. Obviously this will change over time. But if your baby is already in a pattern of one sleep mid-morning and another after lunch, it is a good idea for the minder to know.
- Particular likes and dislikes. Does the child use a comforter? Does he have a preferred sleeping position? Are there any foods to which he has an allergy or a strong dislike? (Make sure you don't give too long a list here. The child may happily eat with the childminder all kinds of things he refuses at home!)

Again, don't be misled into thinking that written documentation of this kind gives you any particular protection against an incompetent or dishonest childminder. The success of your arrangement will in the end depend on the talents of the woman you have chosen, how you relate to her – and on a good deal of luck. But it does help to spell things out before you start. It forces you to raise issues that you might otherwise overlook. And it provides some ground rules for later, if things do begin to go wrong.

THE START

Views differ on how to start a child off at a childminder. Some people favour the brutal approach. You take the child along on the first day and leave it there. It soon gets used to the new environment. This *may* work for some kids. But both mothers and minders feel happier with a more gradual introduction. Perhaps the best way is to leave it to the child. That is, the child and mother come along *together* until it is clear that the child is happy to get on playing without the mother – or until the mother can go away for trial periods without causing real distress in the child. Every child is different in this respect. The breaking -in period can take as little as a morning or as much as two weeks. But unless you are prepared to be very tough, don't take the baby to the minder for the first time on the day you are due back at work. Give him a couple of weeks with the minder before you have to leave him there full-time.

It may well be worth inviting the childminder to your home some time near the start of your minding arrangement. It will help her deal with your child if she knows how he lives at home. And from the child's point of view, it gives him a bit of a chance to get to know the minder on his own familiar territory.

Don't be *too* soft-hearted. In particular, don't worry about the success of the arrangement just because the baby cries when you leave – especially in the first weeks. The minder will probably tell you that the crying only lasted a few minutes. Believe her. She's almost certainly right. You need only start to get worried if the baby always looks very distressed when you come to pick him up – or, maybe, if the tears when you leave don't stop after six weeks or so. But still remember, some happy well-adjusted kids will *always* cry for a few minutes when the parent walks out. Yours might be one of those. Ask the opinion of the minder.

MAKING IT WORK

Let's suppose that you have found a childminder who seems caring and competent and who is well recommended by people you trust. There are now just two pieces of general advice that will help you make your arrangement work. First, always try to see things from the minder's point of view as well as your own. Obviously *you* are busy. But so is she. Think about the strains and stresses on her and how you can make them easier. Secondly, don't ever let yourself imagine that you are paying for a nanny, devoted to your child alone. The minder has other kids to look after. Don't suppose that the interests of yours will, or should, always come first.

The minder has a pretty hard life. She is ill-paid for the very demanding work that she does. Not only does she have other people's children during the day, but she probably has her own kids morning and night. She'll certainly want to have some energy left to devote to them. But on top of that there are all the everyday chores *and* her partner. Be considerate!

- Don't be late paying the fees. Minders need the money. They find it very irritating when their mothers always seem to 'forget' their cheque book on a Monday morning.
- Be punctual collecting your child. When the evening comes your minder might want to go out or spend some time with her own family. Don't abuse the fact that she's working from home, so seems always to be on the spot.
- Don't expect her to devote every hour of the day to stimulating the kids. Obviously you do expect her to do more than dump them in front of the television. But the atmosphere of childminding aims to be rather like a normal home day. Just like you, if you were staying at home, the minder will use part of the day to get on with her regular household tasks. Don't confuse a minder with a hot-house day nursery!
- Don't send your child when he is ill. It is not fair on the minder or the other kids, if he is (as is likely) infectious. And it is not fair on the sick child either – who will feel much happier in his own home. Convalescence, on the other hand, is a different matter. One great advantage of a childminder over a nursery is that the childminder is normally happy to take a child when he is getting better, but still not on tip-top form. Unlike a nursery, she can arrange a quiet day for the child, a bit away from the rough and tumble.
- Make sure that you send your child with a spare set of clothes (two spare sets for a baby or very messy toddler). And dress him sensibly. Childminders get annoyed if they have planned a trip out to a playgroup – but one child has come with slippers on his feet and no outdoor coat.
- Always find time to talk to your childminder – at least several times a week. And take what she says about your

child seriously. She is with him more of his waking hours than you are – and she has probably got more experience of pre-school children than you have.

- Don't try to interfere with your minder's choice of other kids. That is her business. Minders regularly complain that their mothers attempt to dissuade them from taking on another child – or from taking on a child much younger than their own. Remember, in the end you are only one client. You wouldn't try telling a school headmistress or an accountant who they should take on. Don't do it with a minder.

PROBLEMS

How to recognise problems

Even if you have a fairly close relationship with your childminder, you will know very little in detail about what goes on when your child is out of your sight. For the vast majority of people this will turn out to be no real worry. It will be obvious that their child is having a very happy time at his minder's. But – rare as it is – how can you tell if things are going wrong? How can you know if the child is not really settling down? Or is not getting enough attention?

As with nannies (see p. 149), intuition is probably the best guide. If you *feel* unhappy about the arrangement, if you find yourself worrying about the child during the day – share your worries with a friend. Ask her if she thinks you have cause for concern, or whether you are just being a neurotic mother. If she confirms your anxiety, you can probably assume that all is not well.

Intuition apart, there are some warning signs that you should look out for. None is a sure indicator that something is wrong with the minding. But they should all make you think a bit more carefully about what is going on.

- If the minder tells you that your child sleeps a lot during the day, this could indicate that he is becoming withdrawn – in reaction to a situation in which he is unhappy.

- If the minder *always* says that he has been 'good', beware. Either she is not being honest with you – no normal child is good all the time. Or he is *passive* rather than *good* – again a sign of withdrawal and depression.
- If the child is consistently more aggressive at the minder's than at home, it may be that he is not sufficiently occupied, or that the arrangement does not suit him in some other way.
- If the child is always up and full of energy very much later in the evening on the days he is minded, again suspect that he does not have enough to do. Don't blame the minder just because you have a sleepless child. But do take his sleeping patterns seriously if he is regularly in bed at 7 at the weekend, but not till 11 pm on weekdays.

How to solve them

A few problems can be solved. Occasionally something quite simple (like difficulties with potty training) lies behind the trouble. If you have a fairly open relationship with your minder, you should be able to identify this and talk it through. Likewise with the problems of getting settled at the beginning of the arrangement. An experienced minder should be familiar with these. Don't conceal your worries from her. Take her advice seriously. And be reassured that almost all children do get settled, even if it takes several weeks.

For most other, bigger, problems the outlook is pretty gloomy. Try to raise them with your minder. But don't be over-optimistic that you can put things right. If it does turn out to be the case that the child is not getting enough attention, it is very unlikely that your minder will consistently and enthusiastically give him more – simply because you suggest it. One of the consequences of being a 'client' of the minder is this: if you don't like the service you are being offered, you leave.

*

Childcare outside your own home is quite different from childcare inside your home with a private nanny. Expense aside, some people will always prefer the convenience of simply being able to walk out of the front door, leaving their child (still in her pyjamas) to the care of the nanny who has just walked in. Others like the routine of going out to work *with* the child – leaving him with his carer and picking him up on the return home. That's a businesslike working day; and home remains home, private space, not invaded by nannies and hordes of unknown children while you are at work. If you are one of those who prefer the idea of outside care, you ought now to read the next chapter, on day nurseries, and consider that option alongside childminders.

10

Day nurseries

Day nurseries are the least *daunting* option in childcare. This is not because they are more reliable than nannies or childminders. Some are excellent. But some are perfectly dreadful. It is rather that in a day nursery you will have the support of lots of other parents. Choosing a nursery is not like choosing a nanny. You won't have to rely on a couple of, maybe unreliable, references. You will be able to ask friends about the nurseries their kids are actually attending. And when you *have* chosen a place for your own child, you will almost certainly get to know the other users. And you will turn to them first when you are concerned about some aspect of the nursery care – or (more often) when you don't know if you *ought* to be concerned. The 'community of parents' can be a great advantage.

The main problem with nurseries is the great shortage of baby places (that is, places for the under-twos). Social Services Departments apply rather more stringent standards to nursery provision for babies than for toddlers. And they demand a very high staff:child ratio – maybe as much as one member of staff for every two children less than a year old. In addition, it is the official line in most Departments that babies under two are best looked after in a home environment, either with a nanny or (more commonly) a childminder. What lies behind this official policy is not entirely clear. It is, of course, a convenient policy for both Local Authorities and central government. The more you advocate *home* care for the very young, the less argument there is for providing any money for state-run day-care. And the more you can rely on cheap, private, underpaid and under-subsidised childminders.

But from your point of view, it may mean that you have to consider another option in childcare before you can get your baby a nursery place.

THE VARIETY OF FACILITIES

When you start out looking for a full-time nursery place for your child, you may think that a day nursery is exactly the same of a nursery school – or that a creche is the same as a playgroup. Confusingly, this is not the case. Something which calls itself a 'nursery school' will normally operate only during school terms (and will not normally take under-twos, or even under-threes). This is obviously a non-starter for a fulltime working mother, unless perhaps she is a teacher. The same goes for a 'nursery class', which is a separate class for three- and four-year-olds attached to a local infant school. 'Playgroups', on the other hand, are just what they claim to be – mostly rather more casual groups run by playleaders and parents, bringing children together for *play* for up to five sessions of a couple of hours a week, again during termtime. All these may provide a useful *extra* to another form of full-time care (a nanny or childminder). They can't replace it.

The full-time working mother needs a 'day nursery' or 'creche'. Most day nurseries offer all-day care for up to fifty weeks a year. They are not *schools* in any strict sense. Many of the better ones do teach the older kids pre-reading skills and some basic numeracy. But their main purpose is to provide a caring, supportive and stimulating environment for babies and young children to spend a large part of their waking hours. 'Creches' are much the same thing. But people usually think of creches as offering care to young babies (which not all day nurseries do). 'Creche' is also commonly the term used for nurseries attached to offices, factories and workplaces.

Even the single category 'day nursery' includes a variety of different types of organisation – funded in different ways and aimed at very different groups of children.

State day nurseries

Most people can give up any hope of getting their child into a state day nursery. The provision of nursery places by Local Authorities is terribly inadequate, particularly for under-twos. And in practice most nurseries restrict their intake to those children in special need – those from deprived backgrounds, kids whose parents are seriously ill or the emotionally disturbed. If you are a single parent, you may qualify. But just 'being a working mother' will almost certainly not be enough to get you a place.

If you do get a place in a state day nursery, you will find that the fees are very low or even non-existent. You may, in fact, be means-tested to assess your level of contribution. As with all forms of childcare, the quality of these nurseries varies. You certainly can't assume that because they are run by the Local Authority, they are necessarily good. But the best will be excellent, more likely to be in a purpose-built building than a private nursery, and open during hours that will suit a working mother – perhaps as long as 7.30 am to 6.00 pm.

Private day nurseries

Private day nurseries are, of course, even more varied than those run by the Local Authority. But the Social Services Department registers nurseries in much the same way as it does childminders, so some common standards are enforced. Departments are most of all concerned with basic safety and hygiene requirements, and with the ratio of staff to children. Different departments will enforce slightly different figures. But there will always be a sliding scale – with more staff required for the youngest (one to two or three for the under-twos), fewer for the older children (perhaps one to six for the four- and five-year-olds).

Private nurseries are run by all kinds of different organisations. Some are straightforwardly profitmaking. These might be on a small scale in a 'home nursery', with seven or eight kids – rather like an expanded childminder's. But there are also bigger commercial organisations engaged in setting up nurseries. Although 'nursery chains' are much commoner in the USA than here, some firms are beginning to see nurseries as a profitable service industry; there is already, for example, a string of 'Beck Kindergartens' in a number of towns in the South (Maidstone, Beckenham, Wellingborough, Farnborough). Other day nurseries are run by charities or trusts, often established by local groups to fill the need for day care in the community. These nurseries tend to be much more in the control of the parents, who will take some of the places on the 'Committee of Management' and will be involved in fund-raising and policy decisions.

Fees charged by nurseries are as varied as the nurseries themselves. There are two basic rules. First, you get what you pay for. A nursery with very low fees is going to have less money to spend on equipment and on staff salaries. It will have more untrained (and therefore cheaper) staff and the turnover amongst them is likely to be high – as they leave to take better-paid jobs elsewhere. Secondly, babies will be more expensive than the over twos. Because of the required ratios, most nurseries will charge more for the very young. A toddler is commonly charged only two-thirds the fees of a baby. This may mean that the difference in cost between a (say) a nanny and a nursery place for a baby is not as much as you would expect. A good nursery place may cost well over half what you would pay for a nanny. With two kids a nanny may actually work out cheaper.

Of course, high fees do not necessarily mean a good nursery. In a commercial organisation the money may not be going to the salaries of the staff but to the profits of the owner. And even in a charitable nursery, inefficiency or bad adminis-tration may mean that the money is not being well spent. But unless there is evidence of really active fund raising or a hidden subsidy (like free premises), you should *always* be suspicious of nurseries that look cheap.

Workplace nurseries

Some businesses have established creches 'on site' for the children of their employees. These are often set up with the particular needs of the business and its workers in mind. Some of the best provide full cover for both early and later shifts, or for work into the evening. Opening times past 9.00 pm are not unknown. As always the quality of the care varies. But in the relatively small community of a workplace, it is likely that the nursery will *have* to take note of the views and suggestions of the parents using it.

Many firms provide the service of a creche free, or at least heavily subsidise it. But remember, current tax law treats this as a 'perk', and so you will pay tax on the whole cash value of the subsidy. If you want more information on this (and on the campaign to end this tax on childcare), get in touch with the Workplace Nurseries Campaign or your own union.

Workplace nurseries are set up first and foremost for the benefit of parents in one particular organisation (or sometimes group of organisations). But if they are not full, they will sometimes take other local children to make up their numbers. So don't forget workplace creches when you are looking at the local daycare provision – even if you are not a member of the firm concerned.

CHOOSING A NURSERY

Often the choice of a day nursery is a very straightforward task. Suppose all your friends send their kids to one particular nursery and they all speak very highly of it. Or suppose that your workplace runs a very successful creche. This will pretty well make your mind up for you. You should still go and see the place for yourself and meet the staff at least once before your child starts. But other parents are usually a good guide – better than any number of prospectuses and a quick twenty-minute visit.

But do bear in mind the following points:

- Don't trust the recommendation of just a *single* friend or colleague. Some people will have wildly different standards from your own. The thing to take seriously is *consistently* good reports from a number of people whom you know well.

- Make sure you get on the waiting list early – while you're pregnant, if you want a baby place. Good nurseries are always oversubscribed.
- Have a second string. You can never be absolutely certain that a nursery will still exist in six months' or a year's time. Or the waiting list may move much more slowly than you were promised. Or a change of head could mean that it suddenly changes its character. If you are relying on a nursery place to return to work, put yourself on the waiting list of a second nursery. It will only cost a few pounds and is well worth the peace of mind. And to be on the safe side, have some plans ready in case you cannot get your baby into *any* nursery as soon as you would like.
- If you are considering a workplace nursery, think whether you are at all likely to change your job over the next few years. There are obvious advantages in having your baby in the same building while you work (convenient breast-feeding, for example). But these may be offset by the disruption of having to move your baby, when he is very happily settled at eighteen months.

Visiting nurseries

You may not, of course, have a circle of friends who can give you advice on the good nurseries. Or you may be new to the area. In this case you will have to embark on quite a large number of visits to find a place that you like. You will also have to start early if you intend to return to work soon after the baby is born. Even if it seems like tempting fate, you certainly can't afford to leave the planning until the child has arrived.

The procedure is quite simple. Get in touch with your local Social Services Department (under-fives adviser) and ask for a list of day nurseries in your area. Give a good number of them a ring and ask them to send you any information they have about themselves. Some will produce quite elaborate prospectuses. Others will just have a xeroxed sheet. Don't be too impressed by the glossy versions. It is the *information* they give that counts.

Choose a selection to visit. You will be able to rule some out on the basis of the prospectus. Maybe they don't take babies. Or the hours won't suit. Aim to go and see at least three or four of the 'possibles' that are left, especially if you have not much idea of what to expect in a day nursery. One visit may be enough to decide that you want to go on the waiting list. But you will certainly need to visit again before you finally confirm your place. Even more so, if there is a long gap between your seeing the nursery and the baby starting. Nurseries can change quite a lot in nine months.

Make your appointment by telephone. This will give you some idea of the style of the 'head teacher' (sometimes called 'matron') of the nursery. Try to be accommodating about when you visit. A nursery day can be pretty hectic and you will want the head to be free enough to talk. But make sure that you go when the kids are there. And try to sense whether you are being offered a time when the nursery will be untypically impressive (perhaps when half the children have been taken off on an outing)!

You will be looking for many of the same qualities in a nursery as you would in a childminder and her home – safety, good provision of equipment, outside play area (see pp. 170-1). And many of the questions you ask the head will be the same as you would ask a potential nanny or childminder – What are their views on potty training? How do they discipline children? etc (see pp. 169-70). But there are some particular things you might like to observe or ask when you go on a nursery visit:

- What is the training of the head and how long has she been there? How many of the staff are trained NNEBs? How long do they normally stay? This should give you some idea not only of the *continuity* of care your child will receive, but also of the amount of money the nursery is putting into its most valuable asset – its nursery nurses.
- Who actually runs the nursery? Is it a profit making organisation or a charity? Is there a management committee which includes parents? You may feel, of course, that you would never have the time to be a

member of such a committee. But it does indicate that the nursery is likely to respond to the needs, views and comments of the parents.

- Ask about the staff:child ratio. Then do a quick count yourself. If it doesn't seem close to what the head has said, ask why. Some nurseries are almost always short of staff. This will have a direct effect on how much attention your child gets when he is there.
- Study the prospectus carefully before you go. Most give you some idea of the structure of the nursery day. Check if they are doing what they say they should be doing at this time. If the television is still on and it is a good three-quarters of an hour since Playschool ended, be a bit sceptical about all the 'creative painting' and 'water play' that the prospectus talks about. (Perhaps better to avoid nurseries with televisions entirely!)
- How far is the nursery schedule arranged around the convenience of the staff? You will hear a lot of nursery heads talk about how essential it is for the children to have a good rest after lunch. Maybe. But isn't that hour-long nap planned just as much for the convenience of the staff, who want *their* lunch break? Of course, there's nothing wrong about that in itself. The staff, after all, have to have their lunch. But watch out for 'quiet sessions' or television being planned *only* for staff convenience.
- How *consistent* is the care? Does each child have one particular staff member to whom he can regularly turn for help, comfort and advice? Some children get disorientated if their carers change *every* couple of hours – Jane this morning, then Keri, then Linda this afternoon, and so on.
- How is the place decorated? Is lots of the children's work around the walls? And is it nicely displayed and labelled? The quality of the display is important for two reasons. First, it is quite a good indication of the training of the staff. Good, trained staff will have learnt about lettering and presentation. Secondly, it is important for creating a pleasant environment for the children to be in. Few private nurseries are in purpose-built accommodation. They have taken over private houses, church halls or cricket pavilions.

This can be fine – there is nothing *necessarily* good about a gleaming new designed nursery. But you should expect the premises to have been made attractive for the children, however unprepossessing they were to start with.

- Is food served at lunch-time, or do children bring packed lunches? If there *is* food, is it cooked on the premises? And how healthy a diet is it? Watch those 'nursery puddings'! And be careful about places that admit to giving the kids 'squash' (loaded with sugar and artificial colourings). They obviously don't know, or don't care, about modern views on the care of teeth.
- What is the general practice for feeding babies? If you intend to go on breast-feeding while your child is at the nursery, you must find a place that will positively welcome you doing that. It is all too easy for the nursery staff to disrupt your feeding pattern by filling the baby up with juice (see pp. 48-9). And they can also make you feel a bit of an intruder when you come to feed. That can spoil the whole experience for you.
- Will your child's Health Visitor be able to visit him in the nursery, if she wants? If he is having any other medical or para-medical help (such as speech-therapy), will that be able to take place in the nursery?
- What is the general atmosphere of the place? Do the kids seem occupied? Are any wandering aimlessly, clearly with nothing to do? Are any fighting? Are any crying? The key consideration here is the reaction of the staff. Of course, there will be kids crying and fighting in every nursery (just as in every home). But how are the staff handling it?
- Do you feel at ease with the head? How does she seem to relate to the staff and children in the nursery? Does she know the names of the kids? Do they seem to relate easily to her? Remember, if there is any problem it will be the head you are dealing with. So you need to feel that you can get on with her.
- What is the nursery policy on 'siblings'? If you think you might have another baby, you will want to know that the nursery gives priority in places to the brothers and sisters of its existing children. If you are working full-time, you won't

be able to take one child to one nursery, and the other child to another nursery in the opposite direction!

- What about the fees? The prospectus will almost certainly give some information about current charges. But how often do they go up? Is there any reduction for days off?

Remember, the most important question is one to ask yourself: would I feel happy if my child was at this nursery? No checklist of questions will ever be able to answer that. The place might have the answers 'right' every time, but you still feel uneasy. If that is the case, trust your instinct. Don't use that nursery.

COMMUNAL CARE

There are pros and cons about any communal system of childcare. Don't be fooled by those people who mutter that it is 'unfair' to put young babies and toddlers into an institution. It is entirely accepted standard practice in several other European countries. But do remember that using a nursery, and being just one parent out of many, is very different from hiring a nanny or using a childminder.

The main difference is that when you sign up at a nursery you are entering a system that already exists. It is not being set up either *for* or *around* you. There are advantages in this. You are more distanced from the day-to-day organisation. You are, in a sense, a customer whose obligation is to pay the fees as demanded – but not to deal with the problems of tax, insurance, sick-pay or whatever. In the crudest terms, a nursery is a service industry and you are paying for that service, as you would for any other. Many people like that kind of straightforward arrangement.

The other side of the coin, though, is that you have very little opportunity to change the way things are done in the nursery, to suit your own views or convenience. Suppose your chosen creche starts potty training at twelve months, but you would rather leave all that till your little boy seems 'ready'. It may be that the nursery will make an exception of your child if you ask them, and leave him until *you* decide the moment. But the chances are that their attitude will be firmly, but politely: 'This is the way we do it here. We can't run different systems for every child. If you really don't like it, then find another nursery.' Many popular nurseries could fill their places three times over. It is a seller's market – and the 'system' is likely to win.

This problem can arise forcefully over sleeping patterns. Almost every nursery insists on a midday sleep (or, at least, rest) for all its children. It gives the staff a break – and no doubt keeps the kids sweeter-tempered during the afternoon. Many parents complain that this midday sleep gives their two-year-old enough energy to keep going until 8.30 or 9 pm, and they would prefer she did not have it. But what nursery could manage without it? Here lies a major difference between nursery and nanny. You can expect that your nanny will keep your child awake all day if you ask her reasonably and explain. You cannot expect that kind of individual treatment from a nursery.

The other side of nursery life that parents often comment on is the companionship and sociability. It is certainly the case that kids who attend nurseries learn about relating to other children earlier than their counterparts who are looked after individually. It is also true that, at the best nurseries, they learn about friendship in a uniquely favourable setting – equipped with more toys, swings, puzzles and climbing frames than any one home would ever possess. Many parents are delighted at the opportunities the nursery offers their kids.

But remember that companionship inevitably brings illness with it. It is not the nursery staff who will get ill (at least not all at once), so you won't have the 'sick nanny' problem. But your child's illnesses will more than compensate for that! Infections – from measles and chickenpox to varieties of unidentified viruses – pass through day nurseries like wildfire. And no sick child will be welcomed there. They will not be up to coping with the rough and tumble of nursery life, and they will be liable to pass on whatever they have to even more kids. You can be pretty certain that your child will have to be absent for periods of a couple of days at least six times a year – and more when he first starts. So you must have some back-up arrangement worked out in advance, if you are very keen not to take time off work. And if you are moving from a nanny to a nursery, you would be well advised to ask the nanny to stay on for a few months overlap – to have someone on hand to deal with the inevitable first crop of illnesses.

STARTING AT NURSERY

The formalities

The formalities of starting at a nursery are relatively straightforward. You will probably be asked to pay the first month's fees some weeks in advance of your child starting, to secure the place. You may also be asked to sign a formal agreement, stating the regular fees and when they are due – as well as perhaps giving the nursery formal permission to obtain urgent medical treatment for your child and to take him on outings outside the nursery.

Sometime before starting you will be asked to fill in an information sheet. This will include much the same information as the childminder's detailed record (see pp. 174-6) – parents' contact numbers, doctor's name, immunisation details and so forth. But, unlike the minder's record, there will be less interest in your child's minor idiosyncrasies of sleeping or eating. The nursery, however gently, will be trying to incorporate his pattern into theirs.

The first days

Before your child starts at the nursery, you should talk to the head about her normal procedures for introducing a child to the new routine. You will find that practices differ. Some heads like a very gradual process of introduction. You take the child along on the first day and leave him alone for just five minutes. On the next day you leave him for ten minutes, then for fifteen, and so on until he is happy to stay all day. Other heads prefer a cleaner break and encourage the parent to stay only until the child is settled, then to leave for most of the morning – returning, perhaps, at lunch time and leaving again for the afternoon.

It is probably sensible in the first instance to go along with whatever system the head recommends. Don't *insist* on staying for a long time at the very beginning, if it is not what is usually done at the nursery. Give their system a try. It won't do anyone irreparable harm. On the other hand, don't be bullied into leaving your child, if after a few days he is getting very distressed. Talk to the head and explain that you are feeling unhappy and would rather stay with him a bit longer. She will certainly have seen the problem before and won't force you to leave if you really don't want to.

Your problem may be the reverse. Your child may seem well settled – but the nursery is still insisting that he is only left without you for an hour. Do raise this, and say that you would be happy to leave him longer. They may agree. But, if they don't, and they want to stick to their system, it is probably not worth a fight – however aggravating.

Don't arrange to go back to work on the first day your child starts at nursery. Get him started several weeks before you go back. You may be asked to stay with him for quite a long time. And, in any case, the chances are that there will be some kind of upset at the beginning. You don't want to be under any pressure to get to work on time. Besides, it is bad news for your own morale to have to restart work, leaving a howling baby in the care of a stranger. Don't subject *yourself* to that kind of torture. And always remember that babies do eventually get settled. It has been known very occasionally to take up to two months, but it does happen in the end – without any apparent ill-effects.

MAKING IT WORK

Seeing it from the nursery's point of view

Most parents find that they have a ready made support group among the other parents at the nursery. But don't forget the staff. You will find that your arrangements at the nursery work much more smoothly if you try to see things from *their* point of view.

- Do try not to be late picking up your child. Someone (usually the head) will have to stay behind looking after him, attempting to discover where you are. This will not be an easy job. Children tend to get very distressed when left behind in an obviously deserted nursery. Besides, the head will have other jobs to do at the end of the day – and her own commitments after work. If you are late, you are taking up her precious free time, and maybe keeping her from her own kids. Of course, occasionally disasters will happen and you will fail to make it for reasons entirely out of your control. Make sure you let the head know how grateful you are that she stayed behind, literally 'holding the baby'.

- If your child is ill, always phone up to say that he is not coming and why. The nursery will need to know about absentees when planning the activities of the day. And if he has something infectious, other parents will want to be notified straight away.

- Always put a name-label on all your child's clothes. Always send him properly equipped for the day – with a warm outdoor coat and wellingtons, if necessary. Hours of valuable time are lost in nurseries sorting out lost, unlabelled clothes, and kitting out children whose parents have sent them without essentials. Remember, your child is not going to be at all happy sitting inside while the others go out in their duffle coats to play in the snow.

- Do try to pay promptly. It is a waste of the head's time to chase up parents who are behind with their fees. She is not a debt collector, she is a nursery nurse!

- Make sure that you know the names of the nursery staff. Do greet them when you take your child in and *notice* their work. It makes all the difference to the staff when someone comments on the new display of art work, or even on the burgeoning mustard and cress! Most parents probably notice – but they never think to say.

- Don't assume that the staff or the head are constantly available to you. Of course, they will always be ready to talk about urgent problems or to arrange an appointment to talk over things at greater length. But don't go and monopolise the head's lunch break with a series of relatively trivial queries. She probably needs a few minutes rest at midday. And don't pester the staff about your child's 'progress' *every* morning and evening. There are other parents who will want a quick word too.

- Do get involved in some parents' activities. You may not have much time to devote to fundraising or other chores. But if the nursery has an annual general meeting, do make an effort to attend at least that. It is very disheartening for the staff to put on an occasion for the parents, if only a handful bother to turn up.

PROS AND CONS

If you have read right through this book, you will now know the brutal truth: there is no perfect system of childcare for the working mother. A good day nursery has some obvious advantages. It won't close down for a week just because one member of staff is ill. It will give your child a head start in socialising, and will provide him or her with a range of toys and equipment that you could never match at home. But only you can decide how you rate these advantages against the equally obvious disadvantages: the need to provide back-up care when the children get ill (as they frequently will); the tiresome business of packing the children up every morning to deliver them to the nursery by 9 am; and all the jobs the nursery won't do for you – like buying their shoes and their nappies, or getting their hair cut.

In the end it's up to you. So good luck!

Further information

GENERAL READING

J. Bruner, *Under Five in Britain* (Grant McIntyre) A psychologist's view of different types of childcare in Britain (based on a study in Oxfordshire in the late 1970s)

A. Clarke-Stewart, *Day Care* (Fontana) A psychologist's assessment of different types of day care and their effects on the children.

B. Cohen, *Caring for Children* (Report of the European Community Childcare Network – obtainable from Commission of European Communities, 8 Storey's Gate, London SW1P 3AT).

S. Harper, *The Child Wants a Nurse* (Sharper Script – obtainable from Sunny Bank, Roydon Lane, Roydon Road, Launceston, Cornwall, PL15 8DP) A book on childcare (particularly nannies and mother's helps), written by an NNEB nanny.

S. Scarr and J. Dunn, *Mother Care/Other Care* (Pelican). The psychology of working mothers and children, with useful chapters on different forms of childcare.

M. Velmans and S. Litvinoff, *Working Mother: a practical handbook* (Corgi) An encyclopaedic handbook, including chapters on school-age children, how to find work, how to become a childminder yourself.

The Working Mother's Handbook. Short pamphlet obtainable from Working Mothers Association (see below).

USEFUL ORGANISATIONS

National Childcare Campaign Ltd., Wesley House, 4 Wild Court, London WC2B 5AU (01 405 5617/8) A pressure group, co-ordinating campaigns for better childcare facilities. Publishes many leaflets on the practice and politics of childcare.

Working Mothers Association, 23 Webbs Rd, London SW11 6RU (01 228 3757) This association publishes a useful pamphlet on childcare and a regular newsletter. Local branches arrange evening meetings – for working mothers with a few hours to spare!

CHAPTERS 1 & 2

Further reading

G. Chamberlain, *Pregnant Women at Work* (Royal Society of Medicine/ Macmillan). Technical papers on the effects of work in pregnancy.

R. Evans and L. Durward, *Maternity Rights Handbook* (Penguin). Useful guide, but now somewhat out of date on the legal rights.

U. Huws, *VDU Hazards Handbook* (London Hazards Centre – obtainable from 3rd Floor, Headland House, 308 Gray's Inn Road, London WC1X 8DS). An assessment of the dangers of VDUs in pregnancy and more generally.

L. Rodwell, *Working Through Your Pregnancy* (Thorsons). Information on safety and legal rights, as well as exercises during pregnancy, clothes, diet etc.

Government leaflets

Babies and Benefits (FB 8).

Maternity Benefits (NI 17A). A more detailed guide to the rules for different benefits.Both are obtainable free from post offices, Social Security Offices or Leaflets Unit, PO Box 21, Stanmore, Middlesex HA7 1AY.

Employment Rights for the Expectant Mother (Department of Employment, Employment Legislation 4).

Rules Governing Continuous Employment and a Week's Pay (Department of Employment, Employment Legislation 11) Both are obtainable from your local job centre or a regional office of the Arbitration and Conciliation Service (ACAS)

Useful organisations

Equal Opportunities Commission, Overseas House, Quay Street, Manchester M3 3HN. Monitors the operation of the Sex Discrimination legislation and investigates cases of discrimination. Publishes various pamphlets on maternity rights, including *Parenthood in the Balance* and *I want to work, but what about my job?*

Freeline Social Security 0800 666555. A free telephone enquiry service for all Social Security problems.

Maternity Alliance, 15 Britannia Street, London WC1X 9JP (01 837 1265). Publishes *Working Parents' Rights* (a discussion of the current state of maternity provision in Britain and proposals for the future) and *Pregnant at Work* (regularly updated leaflet on benefits and your rights at work).

National Childbirth Trust, 9 Queensborough Terrace, London W2 3TB (01 221 3833) (and local branches, see phone book).

CHAPTER 3

Further reading

A. Price and N. Bamford, *The Breastfeeding Guide for the Working Woman* (Century).
Breastfeeding – Returning to Work (National Childbirth Trust – obtainable from the address given above).

Useful organisations

La Leche League of Great Britain, BM 3424, London WC1V 6XX (01 404 5011).

Manufacturers and suppliers of breast pumps

Cannon Babysafe, Ashley Road, Tottenham, London N17 9LH
Egnell-Ameda Ltd, Quarry House, Mill Lane, Uckfield, East Sussex TN22 5AA (0825 67715). Will provide a list of local hiring agents.
Robbins Medical Supplies Ltd, 23 Old Park Road, Hitchin, Hertfordshire SG5 2JS (0462 33368 & 34899).

CHAPTERS 4 TO 8

Further reading

L. Purves, *How Not to be a Perfect Mother* (Fontana). Includes an excellent chapter on living with nannies.

For information on training of nannies

Chiltern Nursery Training College, 16 Peppard Road, Caversham, Reading, Berkshire RG4 8JZ (0734 471847).
Montessori Society A.M.I (UK), 26 Lyndhurst Gardens, London NW3 5NW.
Norland Nursery Training College, Denford Park, Hungerford, Berkshire RG17 0PQ (0488 82252).
NNEB, Argyle House, 29-31, Euston Road, London NW1 2SD (01 837 5458/9).
Princess Christian College, 26 Wilbraham Road, Fallowfield, Manchester M14 6JX (061 224 4560).

Tax and National Insurance

Lloyds Bank Tax Guide (Penguin). Mostly concerned with personal taxation, but helpful for the general rules of an employee's tax.

Government pamphlets

Employer's Guide to Pay As You Earn (P7) (though remember this is not
specifically concerned with the Simplified System of deductions)
Employer's Guide to National Insurance Contributions (NP15)
Employer's Guide to Statutory Sick Pay (NI 227)
All these are obtainable from your local tax office.

Employment legislation

Department of Employment, Employment Legislation Booklets, all obtainable from your local Job Centre or a regional office of the Arbitration
and Conciliation Service (ACAS): 1. *Written Statement of Main Terms
and Conditions of Employment*. 8. *Itemized Pay Statement*. 13.
Unfairly Dismissed? 14. *Rights to Notice and Reasons for Dismissal*
Staff Employment Services, PO Box 16, Shirley, Solihull, West Midlands
B90 3HZ. Will supply pre-printed forms to fill in: 'Statement of Terms
of Employment'.

Insurance

Lyall Eason and Dudley Division, Barnet Gold Ltd, Garfield House, 86-88
Edgware Road, London W2 2EA (01 724 6666). Provide insurance
against negligence and malpractice for NNEB nannies (others may be
covered, but at a higher premium).

Advertising for nannies

Classified Advertisement Department, *The Lady*, 39-40 Bedford Street,
London WC2E 9ER.
Child-Care Classified Department, *Nursery World*, 24/25 Cowcross Street,
London EC1M 6DQ (01 253 1691).

Employment agencies

Most of these advertise in *The Lady* or *Nursery World*, but note also:

Special Care Agency, Kiln Bolton House, Upper Basildon, Reading, Berkshire RG8 8TB (0491 671842). Nannies and other carers for disabled
and handicapped children.
Federation of Recruitment and Employment Services Ltd, 10 Belgrave
Square, London SW1 (01 235 6616).

CHAPTER 9

Further reading

B. Bryant, M. Harris, D. Newton, *Children and Minders* (Grant McIntyre). An assessment of the quality of childminding and its effect on children (based on a study in Oxfordshire in the late 1970s).

Useful organisations

National Childminding Association, 8 Masons Hill, Bromley, Kent BR2 9EY (01 464 6164). Publishes information for childminders, research papers on childminding and leaflets and booklets to help those looking for a minder: *So you want to find a childminder* and *I need a childminder*.

CHAPTER 10

Further reading

C. Garland, S. White, *Children and Day Nurseries* (Grant McIntyre).
K. Sylva, C. Roy, M. Painter, *Childwatching at Playgroup and Nursery School* (Grant McIntyre). Two books from the Oxford Preschool Research Project – particularly concerned with the quality of nursery care.

Useful organisations

Workplace Nurseries Campaign, Room 205, Southbank House, Black Prince Road, London SE1 7SJ (01 587 1546). Campaigns particularly to have workplace creches *not* counted as a taxable perk.

Index